Grab A
Live

By: Cassandra Mack

Grab A Girlfriend & Go
Live Your Dreams

Copyright © 2018, 2015 by Cassandra Mack

2nd Edition

Published by: Strategies for Empowered Living Inc.

About The Author... Cassandra Mack

Cassandra Mack is a trained social worker, successful author, life skills strategist, corporate trainer, and an ordained minister who started her professional career in the social service sector working with youth running afterschool and day camp programs as well as conducting educational workshops and facilitating life skills groups. In 2000 she left her job as the director of youth services for one of the most dynamic social services organizations in NYC to start her own consulting business as a corporate trainer and facilitator for human service organizations. Cassandra's company, *Strategies for Empowered Living Inc.*, is a training and development company that provides training, coaching and consulting to help individuals and organizations maximize potential, build capacity and facilitate success.

Cassandra is the founder of, *Cassandra Mack Ministries,* a ministry that utilizes print and social media to train, mentor and equip people with Kingdom-based empowerment tools for victorious living. Every Sunday she hosts *The Sunday Morning Hour of Power Call,* which is affectionately known as *Church By Phone.*

Cassandra speaks at churches, corporations, clubs, and national conferences. She has written more than ten books that are widely utilized in the human services. Cassandra is the voice of counsel to thousands around the world through her books, seminars, Bible-based teaching calls, Facebook Pages, Youtube videos and coaching programs. For more information visit: **StrategiesForEmpoweredLiving.com**

Grab A Girlfriend and Go Live Your Dreams by Cassandra Mack

Table of Contents

Part 2. Plan It

Part 3. Do It

Grab A Girlfriend and Go Live Your Dreams by Cassandra Mack

Grab A Girlfriend and Go Live Your Dreams by Cassandra Mack

Intro
Why I Wrote Grab A Girlfriend & Go Live Your Dreams

It started with the book, *Grab A Girlfriend and Go Take Your Life Back."* This was the first book in the **Grab A Girlfriend and Go** series. It was a 30-day challenge for women to reclaim their lives from stagnation and purposelessness. It was written for who felt like they were stuck in a rut and needed to revamp their lives in a more targeted and intentional way. The whole premise behind the first Grab A Girlfriend and Go book as well as the Grab A Girlfriend & Go movement was about harnessing the power of sisterhood by way of bringing like-minded, positive women together to encourage each other and hold one another accountable to living their best lives. Because, when we as women come together to build each other up, support each other's dreams and catch one another when we fall, then not only do we achieve our dreams faster, but we're better able to live our lives from a place of hope, courage, and empowerment.

In this book, *Grab A Girlfriend and Go Live Your Dreams,* you will be taking a 30-day journey into your big ideas, the talents you've been sitting on and most of all ...your deepest dreams. Additionally, you'll be pulling from the power of sisterhood so that you can garner the necessary support to bring your dreams into fruition.

So, if you are a woman with a dream in your heart or a big idea that's been percolating inside your head, my question for you is: *How*

Grab A Girlfriend and Go Live Your Dreams by Cassandra Mack

much longer are you going to wait until you act on your big ideas and dreams?

How long are you going to keep saying that you're going to step out on faith and do that thing that you feel called, led and purposed to do? How much longer are you going to wait to start doing the things that ignite your passion and fuel your soul? How long have you been saying that you're going to: go back to school, start that business, launch that creative project, take the trip that you've been dreaming of, or write that book you've always wanted to write? How many years have to pass you by before you begin to pursue the things that you've been talking about and dreaming about?

How much longer are you going to keep sitting on your talents, your big ideas and your heartfelt dreams? How much longer are you going to wait until you start to live your REAL LIFE ...you know...*the one that you imagine inside of your head?* When are you going to stop holding back so you can show up boldly for your life?

Don't you know how *AWESOME* you are? You were born with a purpose. You were created to illuminate light. You are the embodiment of greatness. You are God's handiwork personified. You have ideas worth sharing, talents worth multiplying and dreams worth pursuing. I know this and you know this ...so what are you waiting for? Permission? Validation? Perfect Timing?

I'm going to ask you again: *How long are you going to wait until you start living your dreams? ...One year? ...Five years? ...Ten?*

The point that I am making is when you say you want a different life, when you have ideas and

8

dreams and visions that you want to bring into fruition, then the time to act on them is now, not later. Because tomorrow is not promised to any of us. The reality of life is ...one day you will wake up and realize that there won't be any more time to get around to living your dreams. And that would be a tragedy indeed.

You have the power to live your dreams right now and here's how I know this: When you have BIG dreams, BIG ideas and BIG plans that your heart and soul long to manifest, you go from being just another woman with a wish into becoming a WOMAN ON FIRE ...who is full of LIFE ...full of HOPE and full of DETERMINATION. You become the type of woman who thinks big, speaks big, takes big action and achieves bigger results. You become the kind of woman who will spin the world on its axis, dance in the rain, skip to your own beat even when you're off beat and then testify about it so that every woman within your sphere of influence knows beyond a shadow of a doubt that if you can pursue your dreams then she can too.

With that being said: The reason I wrote, *Grab A Girlfriend and Go Live Your Dreams,* is threefold: First, to build a springboard for you to jumpstart your dreams. Second, to help you clearly see that with your gifts and talents you can leave your mark on the world and impact others. Third, to help you realize that you are THAT WOMAN who has the power to make a difference and SHINE.

Grab A Girlfriend and Go Live Your Dreams, is for every multi-passionate woman who has something to say, create, craft, teach, build,

9

launch, leap into, generate, birth or become ...but the dream has been locked up inside of you for so long that you can't quite figure out how to make it happen or you know what you need to do but you need a swift push in order to jump off the diving board and go all in.

Grab A Girlfriend and Go Live Your Dreams, is for every woman who is tired of playing her life small and watching other people live their dreams when you should be and could be living your own.

Grab A Girlfriend and Go Live Your Dreams, is for every woman who knows that there is so much more to her life than what she is currently experiencing and she is finally ready to lean in and shine.

Grab A Girlfriend and Go Live Your Dreams, is for every woman who knows exactly what matters in her life and who is on a mission to live her dreams even though it might be scary at first ...and at times she doesn't know what to do or where to start.

Grab A Girlfriend and Go Live Your Dreams, is for women like you and me who live with purpose and according to our own convictions and most of all who are willing to forgo convention in order to take a chance on living our dreams.

Now that we've got that out of the way, let me tell you what we're going to do in this book: For 30-days in a row I am going to coach you through a series of simple steps that will enable you to start working on your dreams right now. With each daily assignment, you will find that you are one step closer to bringing your dreams into fruition. You will also learn how to develop new mindsets and helpful habits that will keep you moving forward in the direction of your dreams.

Just like the first book in this series, *Grab A Girlfriend & Go Take Your Life Back*, you must find another woman to serve as your accountability partner; be it a girlfriend, your mother, your sister, a co-worker, a woman at your place of worship or even another mom if you're a parent. **This Is Important!**

Make sure that you can touch base with your accountability partner at least once a week for roughly fifteen to thirty minutes via phone, text, Facebook or email so you can update her on your progress. This way, you'll have another woman who you can call upon, who will not only cheer you on every step of the way, but will also hold you accountable to the dreams that you say you want to pursue. It's even better if she has up a copy of the book too, this way she can take this challenge with you. At a minimum you need to be able to touch base with her at the end of every module to let her know how you're doing with the challenge, where you need additional support and what progress you've made.

After you complete the program, Post about it on social media under the hashtag: #CassandraMackGrabAGirlfriendAndGo

I can't wait to hear about your progress. Let's go get it!

12

Part 1.
Dream It

Grab A Girlfriend and Go Live Your Dreams by Cassandra Mack

Day 1.
Know That Your Dreams Are Valid

Did you watch the 86th Annual Academy awards? If so: Remember the last line of Lupita Nyong'o's Oscar acceptance speech when she said, *"No matter where you're from, your dreams are valid."* This powerful statement not only affirmed Lupita's decision to pursue her dream as an actress, no matter the obstacles she faced, but it also serves as a reminder to all women that no matter where you're from, what you've been through or how much further you have to go before you finally hit your stride.....*your dreams are valid too.* YOUR dreams are valid because YOU are worthy and deserving of the life you envision.

You are worth the degree. You are worth the house you want to live in. You are worth the beautifully decorated apartment with the great view. You are worth that dream job with excellent pay. You are worth that money-making business that will help others while building wealth for you. You are worth your dream of performing your music or one-woman stage play or showcasing your art. You are worth that great adventure or that once in a lifetime opportunity. You are worth your dream of becoming an author and going on a multi-city book tour. You are worth the loving relationship you want. You are worth a life filled with passion, and purpose and all the joy you can stand. *You are worth your dreams!* Now you say it with me: *I am worth my dreams! My dreams are valid!*

Even though we intuitively know that our dreams are valid, somewhere along the way, our confidence takes a beating, we become skeptical and overly practical, our dreams get placed on the backburner, we become bogged down by the adult responsibilities of life and as a result we stop dreaming and stop believing...which ultimately translates into giving up on our dreams. Then without notice or warning something inside of us emotionally checks out and we begin to realize that we are living pleasant little lives of quiet desperation. You don't have to live this way. You have the power to pursue your dreams.

Did you know that an amazing thing happens when you begin to realize that your dreams are valid? You pursue them with tenacious determination. Even more, you'll naturally connect with people who will encourage you because people are drawn like magnets to those who are pursuing their dreams. Think about the woman who goes back to school at the age of 60 or the single mother who buys a home despite having to support her children with limited resources or the woman who was once a victim of domestic violence and is now an advocate for women: we gravitate toward women like this. Why? Because they are our SHEROES. They inspire us. They show us by example that no matter what life brings your way, you have the power to persevere.

Today, you are going to take a page out of Lupita Nyong'o's speech as well as all the other women who have chosen to pursue their dreams

Grab A Girlfriend and Go Live Your Dreams by Cassandra Mack

no matter the obstacles they faced. Today you are going to validate your dreams by naming and claiming them.

Look in the mirror and do this exercise right now.

My name is: .... *and one of my dream is to.....................*
Another one of my dreams is to..
And another one of my dreams is to..
My biggest, boldest dream that I have never told anyone is.........................

How did it feel to name and claim your dreams? Were you excited? Slightly nervous? Ambivalent? Elated? Hold onto that feeling and in the space below, write down at least 5 things that you have always dreamed about doing or having... and don't hold back.

<u>Here Are 5 Things That I've Always Dreamed About Doing or Having:</u>

1. _____

2. _____

3. _____

4. _____

5. _____

16

Grab A Girlfriend and Go Live Your Dreams by Cassandra Mack

☑ **Your Reminder** – Remember that your dreams are valid. Today is your day to name and claim your dreams. You are worth your dreams. Your dreams are worth having, doing and pursuing.

➲ **Repeat This Aloud** – *Today is the day that I am naming and claiming my dreams. My dreams are valid. This is my time to do and have some of the things that I've always dreamed about doing and having.*

✎ **Journaling** - Reflect on the lessons learned from day 1 of the *Grab A Girlfriend and Go Live Your Dreams* 30-day challenge. Pick up a notepad or journal to be used exclusively for this 30-day program and write down at least one thing that you can do today to put the lessons learned from today's reading into practice. Use your journal to make any notes-to-self, journal your thoughts and feelings about today's task or jot down anything else that you feel prompted to write concerning your *Grab A Girlfriend and Go Live Your Dreams* journey.

Day 2.
No More Hiding and Lying

You know how it goes. We all start out young, optimistic and full of hope. Then as we get a little older, have a few setbacks and experience one disappointment after another, we become more and more discouraged until the voice of self-doubt rings louder than the voice of our hopes and dreams. We start going through the motions and we settle...we settle for just okay rather than happy and fulfilled. And the worst part about it is we convince ourselves that we are okay with living a life that is void of passion, purpose and joy.

If you ask most women: *What's stopping you from living your dreams?* Most will say: *I honestly don't know.* And if you don't know what's stopping you from doing that things that fuel your passion and feed your soul, then how can you possibly live your dreams? You can't. That's why today we are going to focus on the biggest way that we hold ourselves back from living our dreams. And this is not going to be easy for you to hear.

The main reason why you feel held back from living your dreams is because of this one reason and this reason alone: *You are either **lying** or **hiding**.*

Wait A Minute, Cassandra! *What do you mean I'm lying and hiding? I am not lying. I'm an honest person. And I am not hiding. I don't have anything to hide. How can you say something like that?*

Grab A Girlfriend and Go Live Your Dreams by Cassandra Mack

Here's why: Your happiness and success is rooted in you being your most magnificent, brilliant and authentic self. It's about being authentically YOU...authentic to your deepest desires ...authentic to your heartfelt longings, ...authentic to your core purpose ....authentic to your quirks and idiosyncrasies ....and most of all authentic to your intuitive brilliance. And I'm not talking about your job, or the list of things that you want to do before you die, or the goals that you want to accomplish or the roles you play at work and at home. I'm talking about something that goes much deeper. I'm talking about...Your DIVINE purpose.

You came here with a DIVINE purpose. You are a unique and one-of-a-kind soul. There has never been another YOU before. And there will never be another YOU again. This is why no one except YOU will ever fully understand YOU. This is why, more often than not, you feel like YOU are the odd girl out, or the strange bird in the flock. This is why you have a hard time fitting into the box. You were not meant to fit in. You were meant to stand out and shine. This is also why the people that you meet, work with and even some of your relatives may not understand all of the intricacies that make you uniquely YOU. So what I am saying here? Simply this: You have to dig deeper than you've ever dug before in order to find what I call your ...DIVINE purpose ....the YOU that is just beneath the surface of your pleasant little life, the YOU that is dying to come out and play, create and experience a deeper level of meaning and fulfillment.

19

William Shakespeare said it best..."*This above all: to thine own self be true.*" But you can't be true to yourself, if you are **lying** and **hiding**. I am going to explain what I mean by this in a moment.

When you are connected to your most Magnificent Self and you're living your life as *That Woman* your life will change immediately, not in six months or next year but immediately. Because authenticity produces an inner shift at the soul level. When you are crystal clear about what you came to do, why you're doing it and how you can bless and serve others, that's when you become completely powerful in your own skin. You also become unstoppable.

You've got to know without a doubt that your MAGNIFICENT SELF is already inside you, waiting to be released. Your MAGNIFICENT SELF was present with you in the womb, before you were even born. This is why there's a scripture in the Bible that goes, *"Before I formed you in the womb I knew you, before you were born I set you apart."* You were created in magnificence and brilliance. So if you were created in magnificence and brilliance then it would stand to reason that you have a whole lot of magnificence and brilliance inside of you waiting to be released...but you have to stop **hiding** and **lying** so that you can liberate the *YOU* that you were born and purposed to be.

Here are some of the ways in which we **lie** and **hide**.

How We Lie: *Money is not important. I am okay with being broke.*

Why Is This A Lie? Money is important. You cannot pay your bills, buy groceries, put gas in your car or maintain your home or apartment without it. If you're a mom, you cannot raise your children without it. Babies need diapers and children outgrow their clothes. You cannot finance your dreams without it; whether your dream is to start a non-profit for children with special needs, sing on a cruise ship, sell your handmade jewelry, launch your business as a motivational speaker or write your memoirs, all of these things require startup money. *So money is important!* It's not that money is not important to you, it's that you tell yourself this lie because you're either afraid that people will think you're materialistic or you believe that money is the root of all evil, when in fact it's not money that is the root of all evil, it's the *love of money* that's the root of all evil. And there's a big difference between loving money to the point where you will sell your soul for it and recognizing that money is an important form of currency to pay your bills, meet your basic needs and fund your dreams.

What's important to keep in mind is that money is simply a vehicle to pay for some of the things you want and need, nothing more, nothing less. It's perfectly okay to want to build wealth. It's perfectly okay to want to profit from that which you produce. In fact, we are supposed to be fruitful and multiply. So stop telling yourself that money is not important and replace that lie with this truth. *Money is a vehicle that I can use to make bigger and bolder moves. I can be a force for good while building wealth.*

How We Lie: *I don't have what it takes to live my dreams.* (Other variations of this lie include...I'm too old, too fat, too uneducated, too broke, too messed up and the list goes on.)

Why Is This A Lie? *You wouldn't dream of doing it, if it weren't possible for you to achieve it.* There's a big difference between a wish and a dream. A lot of people wish their lives were different but they don't put in the work to make it happen. A lot of people wish that they had the courage to pursue a particular path, but they never try, they just talk, talk, talk. Wishes without action are about fantasy thinking. Wishes without action are about escaping real life. However, dreams backed by action are rooted in real life. Dreams originate from your divine purpose. Dreams emanate from your gifts, talents and your vision for your life. So stop telling yourself that you don't have what it takes to make it and replace that lie with this truth. *If I can see myself achieving my dream clearly in my mind's eye, even if the necessary resources have not materialized yet, then the dream I envision is possible for me.*

How We Hide: *You play down your brilliance.*

Why This Is A Form of Hiding: When you downplay your brilliance, you are hiding because you're not bringing ALL of YOU into the world. What's more is you are living your life from a place of Fear ...FEAR of REJECTION. Fear that people will reject you, freeze you out of their social circle, stop speaking to you, stop liking

22

you, stop inviting you out, totally distance themselves from you and tell everybody who knows you that... *You are self-centered.* Because the truth of the matter is, when you are SHINNING and living in YOUR LIGHT, you will intimidate other women who have not learned how to release their light. And this will no doubt arouse resentment and envy. But here's what you have to keep in mind:

1.) *Light attracts more light...* meaning positive energy attracts more positive energy. So eventually if you just keep shinning you will connect with a tribe of women who are not afraid of your brilliance, because they are busy embracing theirs.

2.) *Light exposes darkness...* meaning when you are operating at your full shine, comfortable in your own skin, doing what you naturally do well and operating from a place of positivism, authenticity and love you will quickly see through all of the BS and toxicity; exposing the haters, naysayers and frenemies. This can be extremely uncomfortable for those who were hating on you on the low. And since most women don't want to be on the receiving end of the type of mean-girl treatment that comes with being envied and resented, we tend to play our lives small in an attempt to appease people who never showed us any real love or support to begin with.

How We Hide: *You allow the things that you're ashamed of to hold you back from putting yourself out there in the most powerful way.*

Why This Is A Form of Hiding:

Whenever we are ashamed of certain aspects of ourselves, or we are hiding something from the past we tend to put up walls and hold back emotionally. The reason we do this is because we are carrying around feelings of unworthiness and inadequacy that stem from our fear of being found out.

Whenever we are operating from a place of fear we are not radiating our best energy. As a result, we will give off an energy of: *being stand-offish, deceptive and evasive,* or *trying too hard to fit in* or *something about our vibe is off-putting.* The thing about energy is, it does not lie. So, people can always pick up on energy, even if they cannot explain what they're feeling or why they are put-off by a particular individual.

The reality is, if your vibe is off, people are going to feel it. They will feel like they can't relax around you or like they need to step back until they can get a better read on you. And this will affect your ability to connect with people who might be in a position to help you.

No matter how you look at it: People can instinctually sense when you are: tense, uptight, insincere, holding back, trying to impress others, when you don't like them or if there's something about your character that's off. And if people don't get a positive vibe from you, then they will not want to be around you. And you will not get the support that you need to take your life to the next level and live your dreams. *Makes sense?*

Speaking for myself, the moment I let go of the FEAR of being judged and rejected, I was able to bring ALL of ME into the room and walk in any

24

room with ease, confidence and grace. And this same lesson applies to you too. Just be yourself, work on the aspects of your life and personality that need improvement... and the rest will fall into place.

So here's your assignment for today: You are going to put an end to the lies and you're going to come out of hiding. You are going to write down all of the ways that you lie and hide, so that you can live your life from your most powerful, authentic place.

How I Lie:

_____

_____

_____

Why This Is A Lie:

_____

_____

My New Truth Is:

_____

_____

_____

How I Hide:

_____

_____

Why This Is A Form of Hiding:

_____

_____

_____

Grab A Girlfriend and Go Live Your Dreams by Cassandra Mack

Here's How I Will Come Out of Hiding:

_____

_____

_____

☑ **Your Reminder** – Today is your day to put an end to the all of the lies that you tell yourself. Today is your day to come out of hiding. You were born to shine. You are magnificent and brilliant. Illuminate your light by speaking truth to power.

➲ **Repeat This Aloud** - _Today I am going to shine. Today I will not hold back and hide. I was created to shine. Let there be light in every aspect of my life. I am a beautiful dreamer._

✎ **Journaling** - Reflect on the lessons learned from day 2 of the _Grab A Girlfriend and Go Live Your Dreams_ 30-day challenge. Pick up a notepad or journal to be used exclusively for this 30-day program and write down at least one thing that you can do today to put the lessons learned from today's reading into practice. Use your journal to make any notes-to-self, journal your thoughts and feelings about today's task or jot down anything else that you feel prompted to write concerning your _Grab A Girlfriend and Go Live Your Dreams_ journey.

Day 3.
Make It Safe To Dream Your Biggest, Boldest Dreams

When I was in my first year of college, I had a professor tell me that writing and speaking was not my forte and that I should consider dropping her class. At the time, I brushed her comment off or so I thought, but looking back, I now realize that sticks and stones may break your bones but words can break your confidence.

Unbeknownst to me at the time, her words were like poison to my soul and they caused me to doubt my ability to live my dreams when writing, speaking, coaching and artistic expression were always the music that played in my soul.

This professor was a dream killer. And as a result of her poisonous words she made it psychologically unsafe for me to dream my biggest, boldest dreams and to utter them out loud. It wasn't until years later that I learned to shake off her words, replace them with words of affirmation and over time I began to dream my biggest dreams again.

When people dismiss your ideas, belittle your dreams or discourage you from pursuing the desires of your heart, they are in fact making it mentally and emotionally unsafe for you to dream your biggest, boldest dreams in front of them. Why? Because a dream needs air and nurturance to thrive. A dream needs to be in an environment where it is fed, supported and encouraged.

Grab A Girlfriend and Go Live Your Dreams by Cassandra Mack

Show me a person who has stop believing in their dreams and I'll show you a person who has experienced a situation along the way where he or she was made to feel foolish, incompetent or not special enough to pursue their dreams. And when you are made to feel stupid, incompetent or just not good enough to cut it, then you will not feel totally and completely safe to dream out loud. This is why today you are going to stand up for your dreams by making it safe to dream your biggest, boldest dreams. *What are your biggest boldest dreams?* Write them down in the space below. And don't hold back!

_____
_____
_____
_____
_____
_____
_____
_____

Now that you wrote down your biggest, boldest dreams what do you need to put in place in order to make it safe for you to share your dreams with others and go after your dreams with bold audacity? Don't over-think this activity. Just write down what comes to mind for you and trust that you know what YOU need to do in order to feel safe enough to dream your biggest, boldest dreams. You've got what it takes to make it! I believe in you! _____
_____
_____
_____

Grab A Girlfriend and Go Live Your Dreams by Cassandra Mack

☑ **Your Reminder** – Today is your day to dream out loud. Today is your day to believe in your dreams and pursue them with persistence. Today you will make it safe to dream like you have never dreamed before, because your dreams emanate from your gifts, purpose and talents. The bigger the dream, the bigger your purpose. It's okay to dream your biggest, boldest dreams. You are finally safe to dream.

↻ **Repeat This Aloud** - *Today I am going to give myself permission to step out on faith and dream my biggest, boldest dreams. Today I will not hold back in any way, no matter how big and crazy the dream, I will say it out loud and use this new line of thinking as the catalyst to boldly go after my big dreams.*

✎ **Journaling** - Reflect on the lessons learned from day 3 of the *Grab A Girlfriend and Go Live Your Dreams* 30-day challenge. Pick up a notepad or journal to be used exclusively for this 30-day program and write down at least one thing that you can do today to put the lessons learned from today's reading into practice. Use your journal to make any notes-to-self, journal your thoughts and feelings about today's task or jot down anything else that you feel prompted to write concerning your *Grab A Girlfriend and Go Live Your Dreams* journey.

Grab A Girlfriend and Go Live Your Dreams by Cassandra Mack

Day 4.
Affirm Your Dreams With Words of Power

Yesterday, you made it safe to dream your biggest, boldest dreams. Today you are going to speak your dreams into existence by affirming them with words of power. Nothing happens unless you speak it into existence. Because everything in life happens twice: First in the spirit of your mind, then in the material or actual realm. Everything that comes into existence begins with a word. This is why the Bible states in the book of John 1:1 ... *"In the beginning was the word."* Nothing was formulated until God spoke it into existence. In the book of Genesis, God spoke and then the thing He spoke came into being. And in the genesis of your mind you have to first call those things that be not as though they are, so that you can develop the strength of mind and the spirit of perseverance to make it materialize.

Our words have transformative power. Words can transform your mood and attitude, from happy to sad or mad to glad. Have you ever been in a bad mood and low and behold somebody came along spoke a word of encouragement and lifted you out of your little funk? If this has ever happened to you, then you know firsthand how powerful words are.

There's a big difference between talking for the sake of hearing yourself chatter and speaking words of power that develop strength of mind.

Grab A Girlfriend and Go Live Your Dreams by Cassandra Mack

Words of power are intentional words. Words of power are positive statements, affirmations, sacred scriptures and mantras that you say out loud in order to get your mind right, build your confidence, encourage yourself, affirm your worth and pump yourself up with the necessary motivation to keep on keeping on. Your words of power can be affirmations from a favorite book or positive statements that you create, or a passage from a sacred book like the Bible. It's totally up to you. The only requirement is that your *words of power* are encouraging and that they propel you to look up, stay in the fight and live your dreams.

Here's why it's so important to speak your dreams into existence by affirming them with words of power: Have you ever said something along the lines of: *I can't do it. I never have any good luck. I will never live the life that I desire. I am a failure. I am so stupid. Nobody likes me. I can't take it anymore. Success is not in the cards for me.* What do you think happens to your confidence and motivation, when you say things like this to yourself, especially when you say them repeatedly? I'll tell you: Your confidence takes a beating and your motivation goes down the drain. And the crazy part about it is you are the one who is serving as your own worst critic, by way of your internal dialogue.

If you're like most people, you probably say more discouraging things to yourself on a daily basis than you realize, even if it's only in the privacy of your own mind via your self-talk. This is why it's vital to monitor your inner dialogue.

You have to be extremely mindful of the words that you speak, especially the words that

31

you say to yourself because our words have living, creative, transformative power. Our words have the power to create and the power to destroy.

More dreams have been destroyed by harsh, critical words, than by lack of talent or skill. You would be amazed at the awful things we say to ourselves when we think that nobody's watching, but YOU are watching and YOU are listening. YOU are somebody. Not to mention, your self-esteem is always at work evaluating your worth and value based on what your mind habitually says to your spirit. So start speaking your dreams into existence by affirming them with *words of power.*

Here are some *words of power th*at I want to speak into your life. Take a few minutes right now to add some additional words of power to this page starting with the words *"I am"* ....

You Are Awesome!

You Are All That!

You Can Do It!

Believe In Yourself!

☑ **Your Reminder** – Today is your day to speak your dreams into existence. Today is your day to affirm your dreams with words of power.

➲ **Repeat This Aloud** - *Today I am speaking my dreams into existence by affirming my dreams with words of power. Today I will respect the power of the spoken word by only speaking the kind of words that encourage, uplift and motivate me. I am somebody. I am destined to live victoriously.*

✎ **Journaling** - Reflect on the lessons learned from day 4 of the *Grab A Girlfriend and Go Live Your Dreams* 30-day challenge. Pick up a notepad or journal to be used exclusively for this 30-day program and write down at least one thing that you can do today to put the lessons learned from today's reading into practice. Use your journal to make any notes-to-self, journal your thoughts and feelings about today's task or jot down anything else that you feel prompted to write concerning your *Grab A Girlfriend and Go Live Your Dreams* journey.

Grab A Girlfriend and Go Live Your Dreams by Cassandra Mack

Day 5
Let Go of Could-Have-Been & Should-Have-Known

Shoulda! Woulda! Coulda! Three of the most self-defeating words that come out of the human mouth. Why do we do beat up on ourselves with these 3 little yet very counterproductive words? Here's my theory: It's because we've allowed regret to steal our confidence and get the best of our dreams.

Whenever we allow the curveballs of life to fill us with regret, the spirit of self-doubt will creep in and slowly eat away at our hopes and dreams. Whenever we compare our lives with other people's accomplishments and accolades; it can make us feel like we don't measure up. As a result, we start to minimize our own dreams. The reason we get so down on ourselves when we play the comparison game, rather than celebrating our own successes is because we are looking at our lives through the rear view mirror of *could-have-been* and *should-have-known.*

And whenever we do this, we become more prone to judging our self-worth and significance from the place of: missed opportunities, past failures, mistakes and personal struggles rather than looking at our lives from the wisdom we've gained, the resilience we've developed and the insight we've acquired that comes from our experiences.

It is very dangerous .... dangerous to your personal growth, peace of mind and most of all to the pursuit of your dreams to base your significance on what *could-have-been* or what you *should-have-known*. Because the bottom and top line is, when you know better, you do better. And now that you know better, you have a responsibility to yourself to show up for your life BRILLIANTLY, MAGNIFICENTLY and AUTHENTICLY as the woman you are today, not the woman you were yesterday.

This starts by letting go of each and every *could-have-been* and *should*-have-*known* core belief that you are still holding on to. Here's how you can begin to let go of *could-have-been* and *should-have-known* beliefs:

Step 1.) Remind Yourself That The Past Is Behind You, but Your Future Is In Front of You.
Whatever you think you should have known or done differently is in the past, it is already done. You can either: continue to beat yourself up about it, or you can forgive yourself and do better moving forward. Why not decide right now in this moment to let it go and move forward? You hold the key to escaping the regret trap. Use your key to open the door to moving forward with hope.

Step 2.) Remind Yourself That The Decision You Made Back When, Seemed Like The Best Option At The Time.
There's a reason we say that, *"Hindsight is 20/20 vision."* The reason this expression is so popular is because none of us can ever fully and accurately know the outcome of a decision we make until we look back at our lives after the decision has been made. We make our decisions

35

based on the information we have at the time. You don't know that you're going to hate your job until after you've worked there. You don't know that a particular business venture was not a smart one, until after you start the venture. You don't know that you should have fought for a relationship or left it sooner, until after the fact. You just don't know what you don't know, until you've had the time and distance from it to step back and process it through the lens of hindsight. So stop being so hard on yourself and let it go.

Step 3.) Channel Your Could-Have-Been and Should-Have-Known Into Now I Am More-Determined-Than-Ever

Speaking for myself, right now, I feel more determined than ever to do what makes me happy and satisfies my soul. This is what motivates me to get out of bed and show up for life as if my life depended on it. Know why? Because my life does depend on me showing up fully. I have lived with could-have-been and should-have-known for way too long and all it ever did for me was make me depressed, defeated and discouraged. And I have too much living to do, too many dreams to fulfill and too many lives to impact to allow regret to rob me of the fullness of life. And the same thing goes for you.

With this in mind, think about your own life and answer these two questions: *Right now, what do you feel even more determined than ever to do? Knowing what you now know, how will you live your life moving forward?* Take some time to reflect on these questions, and then channel your

Grab A Girlfriend and Go Live Your Dreams by Cassandra Mack

energy in the direction of your BRILLIANT, MAGNIFICENT and AUTHENTIC life.

☑ **Your Reminder** – Today is your day to let go of could-have-been and should-have-known. Today is your day to replace regret with hope, renewed vision and forward movement.

➲ **Repeat This Aloud** - *Today I am letting go of could-have-been and should-have-known. Today I am moving forward with full steam ahead. I am moving forward in the fullness of my power. Now more than ever I am going to live my life with Brilliance, Magnificence and Authenticity.*

🖊 **Journaling** - Reflect on the lessons learned from day 5 of the *Grab A Girlfriend and Go Live Your Dreams* 30-day challenge. Pick up a notepad or journal to be used exclusively for this 30-day program and write down at least one thing that you can do today to put the lessons learned from today's reading into practice. Use your journal to make any notes-to-self, journal your thoughts and feelings about today's task or jot down anything else that you feel prompted to write concerning your *Grab A Girlfriend and Go Live Your Dreams* journey.

Day 6.
Protect Your Dreams From People With Short-Sighted Vision

Do you ever feel as though you're holding back how freaking awesome you really are and if the world only knew, the sky would be the limit for you? *It's okay* ... you can admit how awesome you are. Because your awesomeness comes from the fact that you were fearfully and wonderfully made. Guess what else? You can also admit that you have some pretty amazing things that you would like to share with the world. Just like an Eagle you were born to soar. But sometimes when you are an Eagle and you're surrounded by chickens, vultures and dodo birds, you may start to feel as though you have to clip your wings in order to fit in.

But the reality is: An Eagle was born to soar. Instinctively the Eagle knows this. However, sometimes when an Eagle is surrounded by chickens *(people with short range vision who don't know how to fly)* the Eagle allows the chickens to get in her ear and hold her back from taking flight. Isn't it ironic that the Eagle, who is the most majestic of all the birds, will clip her own wings in order to be accepted by a bunch of birds who can't do anything for her except show her how to act like a chicken? A chicken can't even fly for goodness sake...so why are you placing so much stock in what a bunch of birds have to say about you and your dreams.

Grab A Girlfriend and Go Live Your Dreams by Cassandra Mack

If you only recognized your true potency, you would stop hanging around chickens and you'd get around some other Eagles who can see at your level of vision. Not because you're a snob or because you think you're better than other people, but because YOU have places to go, people to meet and things to do. You've got to spread your wings so you can soar.

You are like that Eagle ...meaning you are destined to soar but in order to do so you have to be mindful not to surround yourself with people who cannot see at your level of vision. Otherwise you will end up clipping your own wings and holding yourself back.

My grandmother used to say, *"The people who are in your life do one of three things: They lift you up, keep you where you are or bring you down.* And I am thoroughly convinced that my grandma was right. I've spent a lot of time thinking about how this statement relates to living your dreams and what I have come to know is this: The more that you want to do with your life, the more vigilant you have to be about who you allow in your inner circle and who you share your big ideas and dreams with, because once again ...everyone cannot see at your level of vision.

Everyone cannot handle where your big ideas and dreams are going to take you. Everyone will not be able to understand the changes that you're going to need to implement in your thinking and habits in order to elevate your life and get your dreams off the ground, especially people who knew you way back when...and sometimes this includes friends and family.

Grab A Girlfriend and Go Live Your Dreams by Cassandra Mack

So before we go any further, the question that I want you to answer today is this: *Are the people in your life lifting you up, keeping you where you are or bringing you down?* In essence are you connected to other Eagles? Spend some time thinking about this question and be brutally honest .....because the company you keep can either help you get to the next level or they can hold you back and take you off track. You get to decide who you want in your inner circle and who needs to be kept at a safe distance.

Being selective about the company you keep is not about being judgmental or big-headed. It's about being so clear and intentional about your life, that you refuse to allow people who are not aligned with your vision and who do not have a sincere interest in your success to occupy any real space in your life.

Here are some questions to help you get the ball rolling as you seek to distance yourself from the chickens and get around some other Eagles:

- Who have you allowed in your inner circle that needs to be moved into your broader circle of associates?
- Is there anyone who is so toxic that you need to distance yourself from them all together or only deal with them when absolutely necessary?
- Who have you been listening to concerning your hopes and dreams that you need to stop listening to?
- Is there anyone that you need to stop sharing your dreams with because they simply cannot

Grab A Girlfriend and Go Live Your Dreams by Cassandra Mack

see at your level of vision or handle where your dreams are taking you?

Remember – You are not a chicken. You are an Eagle. Stop hanging around people with short-range vision who don't want to see you fly and who are intent on clipping your wings.

☑ **Your Reminder** – Today you are going to start connecting with other Eagles who can see at your level of vision, because they have a vision for their lives too. Today you will do like the Eagle and spread your wings so that your dreams can take flight.

⟲ **Repeat This Aloud** – *Just like the Eagle I was born to soar. I will spread my wings and fly.*

✎ **Journaling** - Reflect on the lessons learned from day 6 of the *Grab A Girlfriend and Go Live Your Dreams* 30-day challenge. Pick up a notepad or journal to be used exclusively for this 30-day program and write down at least one thing that you can do today to put the lessons learned from today's reading into practice. Use your journal to make any notes-to-self, journal your thoughts and feelings about today's task or jot down anything else that you feel prompted to write concerning your *Grab A Girlfriend and Go Live Your Dreams* journey.

Grab A Girlfriend and Go Live Your Dreams by Cassandra Mack

Day 7.
Revisit Your Childhood for Inspiration

Ever since I was a little girl I loved to read and write. I also loved to sing. Reading enabled me to enter other worlds via my imagination but writing was how I escaped my problems and expressed my thoughts and feelings. As a little girl, I wrote songs, poems, short stories and I even said my prayers by writing letters to God. Whenever I feel like I've gotten too far away from my dreams, I revisit my childhood hobbies for inspiration.

What did you absolutely love to do when you were a little girl or teenager? Did you love to paint, take things apart and fix them, play dress up, speak up for those who were unable to speak up for themselves, travel, cook, dance, play board games, make lemonade stands or something else? The point I am making here is that there are clues as to what inspires you and gives your life meaning if you are willing to revisit some of your earlier hobbies and interests that you may have put on the backburner now that you're all grown up.

Do you remember what your childhood dreams were? Before you placed limitations on yourself and had adult responsibilities. When you were a teenager the world was your oyster. You could do anything your heart and mind could dream up. What did you think your life would be like as an adult when you were in high school or

Grab A Girlfriend and Go Live Your Dreams by Cassandra Mack

college? What dreams and aspirations did you have back then? How did you envision your life turning out?

By going back to those earlier years and to your childhood dreams – you'll be able to push through the blocks, baggage, restrictions, limiting beliefs and fears that you have acquired as an adult. Essentially what I'm saying to you is this: If you can press pass all of the beliefs about how you should be living your life now and what you should have accomplished by now; then you can get real clues as to what your passions and interests are and you can use this as a springboard to start pursuing some of your dreams that you may have put aside or you can dream a brand new dream.

Here's an exercise I want you to do this week. Go for a 15 minute walk, with paper and pen in hand. When you finish your walk, make a list of everything that intrigues, interests or inspires you. Use this list as a springboard to start living your dreams.

☑ **Your Reminder** – Today you are going to go back to your childhood for clues. Today give some thought to what interested and intrigued you as a child.

⟳ **Repeat This Aloud** – *Today I will trust the honesty of my inner child to guide me in the direction of uncovering my purpose and discovering my dreams.*

Journaling - Reflect on the lessons learned from day 7 of the *Grab A Girlfriend and Go Live Your Dreams* 30-day challenge. Pick up a notepad or journal to be used exclusively for this 30-day program and write down at least one thing that you can do today to put the lessons learned from today's reading into practice. Use your journal to make any notes-to-self, journal your thoughts and feelings about today's task or jot down anything else that you feel prompted to write concerning your *Grab A Girlfriend and Go Live Your Dreams* journey.

Day 8.
Come and Get Your Supper

Yesterday you revisited your childhood hobbies for inspiration about the things that bring you joy and ignite your passion. Today we're going to revisit our childhood years again by way of a popular urban sidewalk game called, *Hot Peas and Butter.*

Have you ever played the game *Hot Peas and Butter?* Well, if you haven't, *Hot Peas and Butter* was a game in which the person who was **it** hid a belt and the rest of the kids who were playing the game had to try to find the belt. As each player tried to find the belt, the person who was **it** would let the other players know if they were hot (in close proximity to the belt), warm (getting close to the belt, but not as close as the person who was hot), or if they were cold (nowhere near the belt). And when one of the players found the belt he or she yelled, *"Hot peas and butter, come and get your supper!"* and the other kids had to run back to base before they got their butts whipped with the belt. Now if you are not familiar with the game, it might sound like an odd game to play.

And granted in today's times kids may not be able to play *Hot Peas and Butter* because it might be construed as abuse. Understandable. But if you grew up in an urban community like me, this was just one of many urban sidewalk games that you played as a kid. The object of the game was to find the hidden belt, which was the <u>supper</u> to the, *Hot Peas and Butter.*

45
footer

A lot of us are like the kids who used to play *Hot Peas and Butter* and were looking for the belt. Meaning... We have hidden gifts, talents and abilities that we are not utilizing or that we're underutilizing. And just like the kids looking for that belt, some of us are getting warmer (closer to our purpose). Others are getting hot (right in the midst of our purpose). And then there are those of us who are getting colder with each passing day (nowhere near our purpose) And some of us are afraid to look for the belt that we don't even get in the game; ....because the last time we tried to do something different, big or special, we got our butts whipped. Hence we allowed a couple of butt whippings to force us out of the game.

In many regards, pursuing your purpose is just like the game, *Hot Peas and Butter.* Like it or not, your purpose will whip your butt, because nothing worthwhile comes without a butt-whipping price. There's a butt whipping price that you must pay to pursue your purpose and it's called...**blood, sweat** and **tears.** But you know what? It really doesn't matter if you get your butt whipped on your way to your purpose, as long as you stay in the game.

If you really want to unlock the things that make you great, then you've got to get to the point where even if you get your butt whipped, you will stay in the game. You've got to be willing to pay the butt whipping price that comes with uncovering the hidden belt – your hidden potential, your hidden gifts and talents. Hence the saying: *A closed mouth don't get fed.*

So as you delve deeper into finding your purpose, ask yourself: Am I hot? Am I getting

Grab A Girlfriend and Go Live Your Dreams by Cassandra Mack

warm? Or have I gone completely cold and given up? Always remember that you cannot have your supper without the hot peas and butter. *Hot peas and butter, come and get your supper.* Let's go get it!

☑ **Your Reminder** – Today you are going to do like the game...Hot Peas and Butter and go get your supper. Don't allow yourself to turn cold and don't just settle for simply getting warm. Don't stop until you're hot.

➲ **Repeat This Aloud** – *Today I will pursue my purpose until I'm hot. Even if I get my butt whipped, I won't stop until I am walking in the fullness of my purpose.*

✐ **Journaling** - Reflect on the lessons learned from day 8 of the *Grab A Girlfriend and Go Live Your Dreams* 30-day challenge. Pick up a notepad or journal to be used exclusively for this 30-day program and write down at least one thing that you can do today to put the lessons learned from today's reading into practice. Use your journal to make any notes-to-self, journal your thoughts and feelings about today's task or jot down anything else that you feel prompted to write concerning your *Grab A Girlfriend and Go Live Your Dreams* journey.

Day 9.
How Bad Do You Want It?

Have you ever been in a situation where a friend or family member asked you for your advice, then got angry and argued with you when you gave it to them? Well the other day, I had a similar experience with a coaching client of mine that resulted in her breaking down in tears of frustration and me biting my bottom lip in order to hold back my growing frustration with her.

She was crying because her dream wasn't happening. But the reality was it wasn't that she did not have the ability to live her dreams, the truth was that she was scattered, undisciplined, and unwilling to sacrifice some of the *nice-to-have-now* stuff for the *need-to-get-done* stuff in order to make it happen. And when I told her this point blank, she became defensive. Her priorities were not in order. And when I explained to her some of the shifts that she needed to make, she spent the majority of our session debating me rather than taking in what I was telling her and using it to create the results that she wanted to bring about in her life.

This client of mine wanted to start her own business as a life coach and motivational speaker. She paid me well to coach her through the process, but she was not willing to implement the strategies I gave her, nor was she willing to make the necessary sacrifices of time, discipline and resources. Although she said she wanted to live her dreams, she did not want it bad enough to do the grunt work. Which brings me to the question: *How bad do you want it?*

We've all heard the expression, *No pain, no gain.* And this client of mine wanted all of the gains of a business without going through the labor pains. It ain't going to happen! Why? Because every dream worth having, is a dream worth sweating and fighting for. You've got to fight through idleness, uncertainty, lack of motivation and self-doubt. Plus, you've got to be willing to sacrifice some of the things that are comfortable and desirable so that you can put your energy and resources into materializing your dreams.

So today, I want to talk to you about the sacrificial price of living your dreams. Whatever your dreams in life are...Be they: work related, financial, or relational, every dream worth having has a sacrificial price attached to it. Hence the term: *You don't get something for nothing.* It's the law of reaping and sowing, because you cannot get a harvest from an area that you have not sown in. I want to use the Bible story of Jacob, Rachel and Leah found in the book of Genesis to illustrate this point.

The text goes like this... *Now Laban had two daughters; the name of the older was Leah, and the name of the younger was Rachel. Leah had weak eyes, but Rachel had a lovely figure and was beautiful. Jacob was in love with Rachel and said, "I'll work for you seven years in return for your younger daughter Rachel." So Jacob served seven years to get Rachel, but they seemed like only a few days to him because of his love for her. Then Jacob said to Laban, "Give me my wife. My*

Grab A Girlfriend and Go Live Your Dreams by Cassandra Mack

time is completed, and I want to make love to her."
So Laban brought together all the people of the
place and gave a feast. But when evening came,
he took his daughter Leah and brought her to
Jacob, and Jacob made love to her. And Laban
gave his servant Zilpah to his daughter as her
attendant. When morning came, there was Leah!
So Jacob said to Laban, "What is this you have
done to me? I served you for Rachel, didn't I? Why
have you deceived me?" Laban replied, "It is not
our custom here to give the younger daughter in
marriage before the older one. Finish this
daughter's bridal week; then we will give you the
younger one also, in return for another seven years
of work." And Jacob did so. He finished the week
with Leah, and then Laban gave him his daughter
Rachel to be his wife.

So as we can see from the story, Jacob had
to work a total of 14 years and take on Leah, the
sister he did not want, in order to have Rachel,
the woman he really wanted.

My point to the story is that with every
blessing there is a sacrificial price, whether it's
the sacrifice of time, money, comfort, personal
pride and ego and so on. The reason why so many
people are not living their dreams is because they
don't want the dream bad enough to make
sacrifices for it. There's a reason why Beyonce is
at the top of her game and Oprah is a multi-
millionaire. They made sacrifices.

*Where can it be said that you have to make
sacrifices to achieve your dreams?*

- For example: If you want peace of mind, the
  price you pay is forgiving people who you

Grab A Girlfriend and Go Live Your Dreams by Cassandra Mack

believe do not deserve your forgiveness as well as letting go of the things in your life that bring you drama, even if you really enjoy doing them.

- If you want to be financially well off, the price you pay is investing and saving, even when you want a new pair of fabulous shoes or that cute little handbag.
- If you want to have a fit and toned body, the price you pay is exercise and eating right, even when you rather sit on the couch and eat Oreos.
- If you and your kids are living in your sister's house who you do not get along with but you don't have anywhere else to go, the price you pay is being humble and biting your tongue while you save up enough money to move into a place of your own; even when your sister gets on your last good nerve.

The bottom and top line is, no matter what you want out of life, there's always a cost. And if you are really serious about living your dreams, you've got to be willing to pay the price to get there.

So my question for you is...whatever that goal, plan or thing is that you've been asking for, hoping for, wishing for and praying for...whether it's a new house, your own business, a loving relationship, a better paying job or more happiness and peace of mind ....*How bad do you want it and what are you willing to pay via your time, attitude, habits and resources in order to get it?* Because every dream comes with a price attached to it.

Grab A Girlfriend and Go Live Your Dreams by Cassandra Mack

☑ **Your Reminder** – Today spend some time thinking about what you'd be willing to give up in order to live your dream. If the answer is nothing, then you missed the entire point of today's lesson. There is always a cost when it comes to living your dreams, whether the cost is: giving up a habit, behavior, mindset or a comfort in order to live your dreams.

⟳ **Repeat This Aloud** – *Today I am willing to put in the work to make my dream work. I am willing to pay the price for my dream.*

✐ **Journaling** - Reflect on the lessons learned from day 9 of the *Grab A Girlfriend and Go Live Your Dreams* 30-day challenge. Pick up a notepad or journal to be used exclusively for this 30-day program and write down at least one thing that you can do today to put the lessons learned from today's reading into practice. Use your journal to make any notes-to-self, journal your thoughts and feelings about today's task or jot down anything else that you feel prompted to write concerning your *Grab A Girlfriend and Go Live Your Dreams* journey.

Grab A Girlfriend and Go Live Your Dreams by Cassandra Mack

Day 10.
Build The Kind of Self-Esteem That Can Catapult Your Biggest Dreams

I like to think of the mind as a house with many rooms. Let's imagine for a moment that your mind was a house and in the biggest room of your house, is your self-esteem. And this self-esteem room had a door that you could open at any time in order to invite positive, empowering thoughts in or closed at any time in order to keep negative, discouraging thoughts out. And you were the only one with the key to open and shut this door. What would you do?

Would you invite the negative thoughts to come in and stay for a while or would you shut the door on them as soon as you see them knocking? Well if we look at our self-esteem as the largest room in the house of our minds, then it becomes apparently evident that we have to be vigilant about protecting our mental space from negative thoughts that try to pull a home invasion on our minds so that they can get inside our heads and take what's valuable ...*our self-esteem and confidence.*

Believe it or not, your self-esteem affects every aspect of your life including how boldly and persistently you pursue your dreams. Not only that, your self-esteem also affects how you see yourself. A healthy sense of self-esteem is critical to your success because it's difficult to achieve long lasting success and personal fulfillment if

53

you have a low opinion of yourself and lack the confidence to go after the things you want in life.

Our self-esteem is influenced by many factors including: our childhood upbringing, life experiences, media images, our own beliefs about ourselves and our expectations around how we think the world ought to be. With all of these factors that affect our self-esteem the three most important things that you can do to build healthy self-esteem are: 1.) monitor your internal dialogue, 2.) replace self-defeating beliefs with self-affirming ones, 3.) do something daily to boost your confidence and affirm your worth.

It's important for you to know that nobody feels 100% confident in themselves all the time. Not even the most successful people. Everyone has moments of doubt and insecurity. However, what separates people who have healthy self-esteem from those who have low self-esteem is people with low self-esteem allow their feelings of insecurity to prevent them from going after the things they want in life while people with healthy self-esteem feel the fear and do it anyway.

Our minds work in such a way, that they believe whatever we tell them on a continual basis. If you feed your mind a constant diet of negative thoughts, your mind will begin to believe these negative thoughts. As a result you will make choices based on fear and self-doubt instead of making choices from your place of Brilliance, Magnificence and Authenticity.

However, the opposite is also true. If you feed your mind a continual diet of positive, self-affirming thoughts, then over time you will come

Grab A Girlfriend and Go Live Your Dreams by Cassandra Mack

to believe the best about yourself and you'll act in accordance with your truest beliefs.

When you believe in yourself and approach life from your place of Brilliance, Magnificence and Authenticity you become a powerhouse of possibility. As a result, you begin to tap more of your potential, cultivate your talents; and in time you start to see yourself in a more powerful way. This attitude of confidence, competence and positive expectancy will propel you to rise to higher heights. Always remember that how far you go in life and how happy you are as a person, to a large extent, depend on how much you believe in yourself and how forcefully you act on your positive, self-affirming beliefs.

With this in mind: Who or what are you blaming for your level of self-esteem? Now that you know that you are 100% responsible for your self-esteem once you become an adult, what are you going to do to boost your self-esteem? Additionally, a big part of self-esteem involves liking yourself. Quickly name ten things that you like about yourself and say them out loud. Start with the phrase, *I Like...* and repeat this process until you come up with 10 different things that you like about yourself.

1.) I like..........
2.) I like..........
3.) I like..........
4.) I like..........
5.) I like..........
6.) I like..........
7.) I like..........
8.) I like..........

Grab A Girlfriend and Go Live Your Dreams by Cassandra Mack

9.) I like..........
10.) I like.....

Now don't you feel better already?

☑ **Your Reminder** – Every morning when you wake up, look in the mirror and say something positive about yourself. Do this as often as you need to until you pump yourself up with the confidence you need to build unbreakable self-esteem.

⊃ **Repeat This Aloud** – *I hold the key to my self-esteem. I have the power to shut the door on thoughts that do not affirm my brilliance, magnificence and authenticity. I like myself. There are so many awesome things that I like about me.*

✎ **Journaling** - Reflect on the lessons learned from day 10 of the *Grab A Girlfriend and Go Live Your Dreams* 30-day challenge. Pick up a notepad or journal to be used exclusively for this 30-day program and write down at least one thing that you can do today to put the lessons learned from today's reading into practice. Use your journal to make any notes-to-self, journal your thoughts and feelings about today's task or jot down anything else that you feel prompted to write concerning your *Grab A Girlfriend and Go Live Your Dreams* journey.

Self Check-In

✓ What have you accomplished thus far, since doing the *Grab A Girlfriend and Go Live Your Dreams* 30 day challenge? *(either big or small)*

✓ How do you feel right now about the progress you've made thus far?

✓ Was there any part of the program that you were struggling to follow-thru on? If yes, why were you struggling with that particular part of the challenge?

✓ Write down one thing that you can do this week to move your life one step closer to living your dreams.

Girlfriend Check-In

Now we've come to the girlfriend check-in. Think of your girlfriend check-ins as your weekly power chat where you get to discuss your successes and challenges regarding your *live your dreams* journey. You will do your girlfriend check-ins at the end of every 10-day module. Remember that this is an important part of your progress because it enables you to process the work that you've done throughout each 10-day module with your accountability partner. You should have a pen and notebook handy so that you can jot down any helpful ideas or suggestions that come out of your girlfriend check-in.

Summarize 3 things that you did this week to move your life in the direction of your dreams. Talk about any challenges you have faced. Ask for feedback. Do not argue with your accountability partner. Simply thank her for listening and jot down anything that is helpful and useful.

_____

_____

_____

_____

_____

_____

_____

Grab A Girlfriend and Go Live Your Dreams by Cassandra Mack

Dream Work Check List

1. Know that your dreams are valid.

2. No more hiding and lying.

3. Make it safe to dream your biggest, boldest dreams.

4. Affirm your dreams with words of power.

5. Let go of could-have-been and should-have-known beliefs.

6. Protect your dreams from people with short-sighted vision.

7. Revisit your childhood for inspiration.

8. Do like the game...Hot peas and butter with respect to your purpose.

9. Make sure that you want your dream bad enough to put in the work.

10. Build the kind of self-esteem that can catapult your biggest dreams.

Grab A Girlfriend and Go Live Your Dreams by Cassandra Mack

60

Part 2.
Plan It

Grab A Girlfriend and Go Live Your Dreams by Cassandra Mack

Day 11.
Give Voice To Your Dreams

I don't know where I got the idea in my head, but at some point after getting my Master's Degree in social work I decided that I wasn't going to live a *"normal"* life, so to speak. Sure, I still wanted to get married, have a family of my own, have a nice place to live and travel every now and then, but as far as the whole white picket fence thing, that just wasn't my bag. And what helped me let go of who I *should* be in order to embrace who *I knew I really was deep down on the inside*, was the fact that I was not afraid to dance to my own beat and that I was able to give voice to my dreams in clear and vivid detail. When I was finally able to verbalize without holding back; how I wanted to live, how I wanted to work and how I wanted to feel each day, my life began to come together in a way that made sense to me.

Whether your dream is to make music, create art, become a life coach, write a book or travel around the world and take photographs, the clearer that you're able to verbalize your dreams, the easier it becomes to start living them, because clarity is the precursor to productivity. Don't stop at just naming and claiming your dreams, take some time to describe your dreams in vivid detail. Then, give your dreams a voice by speaking life into them. As you start thinking about the details of your dream, don't let fear or insecurity, or lack of resources ...color your vision.

Grab A Girlfriend and Go Live Your Dreams by Cassandra Mack

Because when you have a dream that is rooted in your purpose, you will learn whatever it is that you need to learn in order to make it happen. So don't let what you don't have stop you from pursuing your dream. Instead just think big and explore all of the possibilities that are available.

Now granted, the road to get from where you are now to where you want to be might be a little difficult at first. But then again it may not be as long as you think. And if it's your heart's desire then it's totally worth it. After all, you only get one life to live.

Below is an exercise to get you thinking about your dream in greater detail. Fill in the blanks and see where your responses lead you. You might be pleasantly surprised to find that not only is your dream realistic, but it's completely doable too.

My dream job is to use my gifts and talents which include _____, _____ and _____ in order to walk in the fullness of my purpose and do what I love to do, which is _____, _____ and _____.

I get to fulfill my life calling of _____ and work in inspiring places such as _____, _____, and _____.

Surrounded by the people I love to work with and for, _____, _____, and _____ ... I use my gifts, skills and talent to solve the problems, issues or needs of _____, _____ and _____.

Grab A Girlfriend and Go Live Your Dreams by Cassandra Mack

My days are filled with impactful experiences such as _____, _____, _____ and I get to do some of my favorite things which bring me purpose and joy, like _____, _____, _____ and _____.

I am finally able to afford the life I want, where I can be _____, _____, do _____, _____ have _____, _____ and contribute _____. I am becoming my most magnificent, brilliant and authentic version of myself and it is evident by_____.

☑ **Your Reminder** – Use this vivid description of your dream to guide you in the pursuit of your purpose. Remind yourself that your dream is completely doable, even if you have to take additional training, learn a new skill or access additional resources to get there.

⊃ **Repeat This Aloud** – *My dream is completely doable. I have faith that I can achieve this dream. In my mind's eye, I can vividly see the details of my dream coming together. I will choose to speak life into my dreams so that I give my dreams a voice.*

🖉 **Journaling** - Reflect on the lessons learned from day 11 of the *Grab A Girlfriend and Go Live Your Dreams* 30-day challenge. Pick up a notepad or journal to be used exclusively for this 30-day program and write down at least one thing that you can do today to put the lessons learned from today's reading into practice. Use your journal to make any notes-to-self, journal your thoughts and feelings about today's task or jot down anything else that you feel prompted to write concerning your *Grab A Girlfriend and Go Live Your Dreams* journey.

Day 12.
Put Your Past In Its Place

Are you allowing your past to hold you back? *Be honest.* If the answer is yes, then it's important for you to do whatever you need to do to loosen the grip of the past so that you can move your life forward with a sense of positive expectancy and hope.

If we are honest, we have all done things that we are not too proud of. We have all made decisions that we would not make again. We have all had things happen to us that we try to forget, but can't. And sometimes when we look back at our lives and mentally replay our experiences, the pain still cuts deep, even though it happened a long time ago. Believe me I get it. But at the same time if you want to close that chapter of your life so that you can start a new one, you've got to look your past square in the eye and put it in its place.

The thing about giving your past more credit than it deserves is that when you give your past the power to define you or hold you back, you live your life from a place of shame, hopelessness, and inadequacy. And if you are living your life from a place of shame, hopelessness and inadequacy, you will not take the type of risks that you need to take in order to step out on faith. You need to know that: YOU are not powerless just because you've been through some of life's storms or even the worst that life has to offer. You are still POWERFUL, because you are still here. But in order to tap the fullness of your power, you've got to put your big girl panties on ...~~no scratch that~~...your granny panties with the worn out elastic and make up your mind that YOU are going to become the most *Magnificent, Brilliant* and *Authentic* version of YOURSELF regardless of your past.

Here is where you've got to make up your mind that no matter what you've been through and how torn up you feel about it; that you are going to keep your head to the sky and live your life FACE FORWARD. Why? Because you can't live your life with confidence, power and hope until you've loosened up the grip from your past.

The thing you need to keep in mind about the past is it already happened and you survived it. See ...When we are children, we have no control over the circumstances that come into our lives and no frame of reference to understand why bad things happen to good people. As children we are not responsible for what happens to us. However, once we become adults, we must learn to separate the things that have happened to us in the past, from the things we now have control over. And the truth is, now that you are a grown woman, you have control over your outlook, attitude and emotional well-being. It starts with making the choice to live your life *Face Forward*. You can choose from this point on to not spend another moment of your life feeling rejected and defeated. Instead you can hold your head up high, go toe-to-toe with the best of them and choose to be resilient.

Each day that you choose to dig deep and find the resolve to press your way though, you are loosening the grip of your past. Each day that you refuse to allow painful events from your past to define, defeat or derail you, not only are you putting your past behind you, but you are beginning to live your life Face Forward. Today, know that no matter what has happened to you and how badly you feel about it, as long as you are alive and breathing, you have the ability to begin again. So today, put your past in its place, get it under your feet, trample on it and bury it and CHOOSE to live your life FACE FORWARD.

☑ **Your Reminder** – If you need to go to counseling or join a support group to put your past behind you, then do so. Do whatever you need to do to empower yourself to start living your life FACE FORWARD.

➲ **Repeat This Aloud** – *Today I am choosing to live my life FACE FORWARD.*

✎ **Journaling** - Reflect on the lessons learned from day 12 of the *Grab A Girlfriend and Go Live Your Dreams* 30-day challenge. Pick up a notepad or journal to be used exclusively for this 30-day program and write down at least one thing that you can do today to put the lessons learned from today's reading into practice. Use your journal to make any notes-to-self, journal your thoughts and feelings about today's task or jot down anything else that you feel prompted to write concerning your *Grab A Girlfriend and Go Live Your Dreams* journey.

Day 13.
Adjust Your Spending To Support Your Dreams

It goes without saying that you've got bills to pay and important things to do with your money. And sometimes this realization makes it difficult for you to see how you can invest in your dreams. Yet and still, you've got to invest in your dreams in order to make them happen. If you don't invest in your dreams, they won't come to pass.

In today's *money-over-everything* culture, many people mistakenly equate the good life with owning lots of stuff. But in your heart of hearts, you know that there's so much more to life than a bigger house or a newer car. And you also know that when it all comes down to it, that you really don't need another pair of shoes or a brand new handbag. *Right?* So investing in your dreams is not about being irresponsible with your money or depriving yourself of some of the fabulousness of life. It's about budgeting for your breakthrough and adjusting your spending to support your dreams.

For me, what it all comes down to is balancing doing what I have to do to pay my bills with budgeting for the things that give me genuine satisfaction and allow me to experience life from a place of creativity, connection and community. But in order to do this, I've got to adjust my spending to match my dreams.

Grab A Girlfriend and Go Live Your Dreams by Cassandra Mack

But, before you can adjust your spending to match your dreams, you've got to adjust your thinking. One thing that I am very conscientious of is how I think about money and how I speak about my finances. No matter what my financial situation has been, I do not SPEAK BROKE – meaning I will not say things like...*I am so broke. I can't afford that. That's too expensive for me.*

Believe it or not, when you say that you can't afford something, you are putting yourself in a passive position, because what you are essentially saying is that: *You are not in charge of your ability to create additional funding streams,* but someone or something outside of you is in charge of how richly you live and how many streams of income are available to you. This kind of mindset makes you a victim of your circumstances. And YOU are not a victim. YOU are in control of YOU.

Now on the other hand, when you frame your money from the position of *choosing* how and where you are going to spend your money, you put yourself in a position of power over your money. YOU are in control! It's not your finances that are controlling you, but it's you taking responsibility for how you utilize your finances. By voicing how you *choose* to spend your money from a position of *choice* rather than a mindset of lack, you become an empowered woman who makes conscientious choices about her money, no matter your income, rather than a woman who feels victimized by her finances. Do you see the difference?

Speaking for myself as an entrepreneur and single mom, I am vigilantly aware of how I speak

Grab A Girlfriend and Go Live Your Dreams by Cassandra Mack

about my money and I do my best to NEVER SPEAK BROKE. Instead, I elect to speak from a place of financial choice by stating what I choose to spend my money on; rather than what I cannot afford. For example, when my son asked me for the latest sneakers, which were well over $150, I did not say we can't afford $150 sneakers. Instead I said, *"It's not smart to spend $150 on sneakers when we have other priorities that come first"*

Other times I will list the alternative: *"Having $150 sneakers might be something you want right now, but it's more important to put more money in your bank account, so that you will have some money of your own."*

If my son asks for something that costs too much or that I don't want to spend money on I will tell him, *"That costs more than I wish to spend on a pair of sneakers, which you will outgrow in a year"* or *"Let's see if we can find another popular sneaker at a better price."* I will also try to help him weigh the pros and cons of his request and redirect him towards our financial goals for the year. Do you see the difference that this mindset makes? It shifts your thinking from powerlessness to in-control and choice.

For every dollar you spend, you need to ask yourself: *What is my expected return on this investment?* If you are paying rent or mortgage, your expected return on that investment is shelter. If you are paying an electric bill, your expected return on that investment is light and gas. If you are paying a life coach to help you personally or professionally, your expected return on that investment is an accelerated path to

71

success and tools for self-mastery. If you pay for a book or an educational course, your expected return on that investment is becoming more proficient and effective in a particular area of your life. Get the picture? And if you cannot get enough of a return on your investment then you should re-think how you are spending money in that particular area. From personal grooming expenses to travel and leisure right down to groceries, before you spend a dime, ask yourself: *How will spending money in this area earn me a return on my investment?*

Here's something else to keep in mind. Something that earns you a return on your investment improves your life like: meeting your basic needs, contributing to your personal wellbeing or the betterment of your family or humanity, peace of mind, health and fitness, happiness, success in life or financial security and freedom.

What I'm saying here is this: You can live your dream of starting that business, writing your novel, selling your art, performing your one-woman-show, traveling around the country as a motivational speaker and so on, but you'll have to adjust your spending to support your dreams. And remember don't think in terms of what you cannot afford. Instead think in terms of: Where do I need to adjust my spending or create an additional stream of income so that I can live my dreams?

☑ **Your Reminder** – Today stop speaking the language of broke. Instead speak from the position of choice. Whenever you feel tempted

Grab A Girlfriend and Go Live Your Dreams by Cassandra Mack

to say the words, *I can't afford this.* Stop yourself dead in your tracks and instead say, *I am choosing not to spend money in this area so I can utilize my money in an area that will give me a better return on my investment.*

⟳ **Repeat This Aloud** – *Today I am going to adjust my spending to match my dreams. I have a choice about where and how I spend my money and I will make choices that make sense for me.*

✏️ **Journaling** - Reflect on the lessons learned from day 13 of the *Grab A Girlfriend and Go Live Your Dreams* 30-day challenge. Pick up a notepad or journal to be used exclusively for this 30-day program and write down at least one thing that you can do today to put the lessons learned from today's reading into practice. Use your journal to make any notes-to-self, journal your thoughts and feelings about today's task or jot down anything else that you feel prompted to write concerning your *Grab A Girlfriend and Go Live Your Dreams* journey.

Day 14.
Feed Your Dreams
With Mini Goals

Today I have something to share with you that is probably going to be the very best thing you've heard all year with respect to making noticeable progress toward your dreams. Especially if you've been working your butt off and you feel like you're not even close to where you want to be.

Here goes.... If you truly want to fly as an artist, a leader and a woman on FIRE, you have to adopt the attitude that you are going to keep on keeping on, no matter how long it takes. But sometimes when your goals are really big and it's taking you a whole lot longer than you anticipated to get THERE, it's easy to become discouraged and prematurely give up on your dreams. The reason this happens is because you're not seeing tangible results quickly enough.

Contrary to popular belief, living your biggest, boldest dreams can take a while. After all this is your biggest, boldest dream. This is why I want you to implement the strategy of feeding your dreams with mini goals. This strategy will allow you to see tangible results frequently and quickly.

For example, if you one of your dreams is to learn how to speak French, you can set a mini-goal toward that dream that is so easy to accomplish that you'll end up surpassing your goal. For example, you can set a goal to learn 5

French words per day. Even on your worst day, you can learn 5 French words per day, and on most days, you'll probably exceed this goal. From there, you can build up to your larger goals. This keeps you actively working on your dreams and it keeps your biggest, boldest dream in front of you.

Or, if you have a dream to sing on a cruise ship, set a mini-goal of learning one new song per week. At the end of the month perform at least one new song you learned, even if you do it for free. Setting this mini goal enables you to feed your dream of singing on a cruise ship with milestones that you can easily track.

In many ways a dream is like an inner promise. And we all make inner promises to ourselves, but more often than not, we don't keep these promises because the undertaking of the dream feels too enormous. Or we think that "eventually" we'll get around to it. Or we think that the dream is unrealistic. But when you break your dreams down into mini-goals, you find that your dreams are not only achievable, but completely doable too. Whatever your dreams are, break them down into mini-goals and you will start to see progress right away.

What long overdue promises have you made to yourself? How can you use the mini-goal strategy to start honoring your dreams in a more consistent way?

☑ **Your Reminder** – Use the mini goal process to tie you over until you get to your big win. This way not only will you be able to clearly see that you are making progress, but also when you

Grab A Girlfriend and Go Live Your Dreams by Cassandra Mack

finally achieve your dream, it will seem like you did it in no time flat.

➲ **Repeat This Aloud** – *Today I will be feeding my dreams with mini goals. By the yard my dreams might seem hard; but inch by inch my dreams are an absolute cinch.*

🖉 **Journaling** - Reflect on the lessons learned from day 14 of the *Grab A Girlfriend and Go Live Your Dreams* 30-day challenge. Pick up a notepad or journal to be used exclusively for this 30-day program and write down at least one thing that you can do today to put the lessons learned from today's reading into practice. Use your journal to make any notes-to-self, journal your thoughts and feelings about today's task or jot down anything else that you feel prompted to write concerning your *Grab A Girlfriend and Go Live Your Dreams* journey.

Grab A Girlfriend and Go Live Your Dreams by Cassandra Mack

Day 15.
Don't Cater To Your Haters

I learned a long time ago that everyone is not going to like you. No matter what you do, whether you're out in the forefront living your dreams or hiding in the shadows dulling your shine; there will always be someone who will NOT LIKE YOU. Some people will even resent you ... simply because you are living life with purpose and choosing to *DO YOU*.

The reality of life is haters are going to hate, because that's what haters do. And if you stop doing the things that make your life rich or if you water yourself down simply because your haters cannot handle you at 100% proof, you do yourself and the people who you are destined to impact a great disservice, because you would not be able to share your gifts, skills, talent and personality with those whom you are meant to inspire and serve. This lesson doesn't just apply to you. It applies to each and every one of us. And the sooner you become more than good with the fact that everyone is not going to like you, the sooner you can spread your wings and soar.

The reason that it's so critical that you do not cater to your haters is because if you do, you'll never live your life in a way that illuminates your most *Magnificent, Brilliant* and *Authentic* self. You will always choose to water yourself down for fear of being judged, rejected, laughed at, or envied.

Imagine if Oprah, Beyonce or Nene Leakes from Atlanta Housewives, catered to their haters.

77

Do you think that they would be living their dreams on the level that they are on today? Of course not, because they would be more concerned with worrying about what people thought about them rather than doing that thing that makes them happy.

If you are serious about living your dreams, then you've got to get to the point where you take your haters with a grain of salt so that they don't occupy any of your headspace – space that can be better used to think, plan, create and work on your dreams.

Never feel like you have to appease or go toe-to-toe with a hater, be it a friend, co-worker or even a family member, because if an individual deals with you from a place of envy and resentment, even on the smallest level, then it means that they are not invested in your well-being and success. And if they are not invested in your well-being and success, you DON'T NEED to concern yourself with what they think.

It's nearly impossible to live your best life if you are catering to your haters. Just accept the fact that everyone is not going to like you so you can shake the haters off.

Truth be told, even Jesus Christ had haters, so if Jesus Christ had haters and He came to spread love and save the world, then certainly you and I are going to have our fair share of haters too.

Today remind yourself that haters are going to hate. Then carry on and do what you came to do.

Grab A Girlfriend and Go Live Your Dreams by Cassandra Mack

☑ **Your Reminder** – Know that haters come with the territory and the more you enlarge your territory the more haters you will have. Simply shake them off and keep moving forward towards your dreams.

➲ **Repeat This Aloud** – *Today I will shake off the haters. I will not allow haters to live in my head. My head space is strictly for positive thinking, planning, creating and manifesting my dreams.*

✎ **Journaling** - Reflect on the lessons learned from day 15 of the *Grab A Girlfriend and Go Live Your Dreams* 30-day challenge. Pick up a notepad or journal to be used exclusively for this 30-day program and write down at least one thing that you can do today to put the lessons learned from today's reading into practice. Use your journal to make any notes-to-self, journal your thoughts and feelings about today's task or jot down anything else that you feel prompted to write concerning your *Grab A Girlfriend and Go Live Your Dreams* journey.

Day 16.
Cultivate Your Very Own
...You Go Girl! Tribe

If your goal is to rock on with your bad self and live your life as the Magnificent, Brilliant and Authentic woman that you were destined to be, then connecting with other Magnificent, Brilliant and Authentic women is an absolute must. You've got to cultivate your very own ... *You Go Girl* tribe.

Remember the song "Girl," by Destiny's Child. There's a line in the song that goes, *I'm Your Girl, You're My Girl, We're Your Girls, Don't You Know That We Love You?* Although this song is about girlfriends being there for each other during a relationship gone bad, what we can also pull from this song, is the importance of having women in our lives who support us, stand by us and celebrate our wins – in essence your very own *You Go Girl* tribe.

I've been fortunate enough to have female friends who I can lean on for support, who cheer me on and celebrate my wins with me. I'm forever grateful to have these dynamic women in my life. They support me and I in turn support them. They are my *You Go Girl* tribe. Every woman needs a *You Go Girl* tribe, especially a woman like you with big ideas and dreams.

One of the most critical components to your success is having people around you who want to see you succeed – people who are vested in your success and who support you in your growth. People you can bounce ideas off of and who you can share your plans, dreams and even your struggles with. Think of your *You Go Girl* tribe as your female dream team. A dream team consists of two or more people who come together on a regular basis, either in person, over the telephone or via email to support each other's plans and goals, brainstorm ways to accomplish these plans and share helpful resources.

Your *You Go Girl* tribe should be composed of women who reflect the different aspects of what you aspire to be. They should be positive, supportive, and unabashedly real. They should make you burst with so much positive energy just by being in their presence. They should make you feel like you can achieve any goal you put your heart and soul into, but they should also keep you grounded to your core so that you don't stray too far from your true self. They should motivate you to step up your game and be a better woman. They should challenge you to show up as your best self. But most importantly, they teach you how to bring your Magnificence, Brilliance and Authenticity into the world.

It's important to understand that no one is an island. You can only go so far alone. You need to connect with other positive people who want to see you succeed and who will encourage you to take steps toward your plans and dreams. Here's the final piece: Be willing to help other women along the way. You cannot expect people to support you, if you aren't willing to support and assist other people too. So think of ways that you can be of service and add value to the lives of others. Whether it's through encouragement, sharing resources and opportunities or making a

Grab A Girlfriend and Go Live Your Dreams by Cassandra Mack

referral, when you invest in your girl tribe, they will invest in you. Who can you recruit for your *You Go Girl Tribe*? If you don't know anyone, where can you go to start connecting with the kind of women you'd like to have as part of your network? Identify four to six women who you can cultivate positive networking relationships with. If you don't know four to six positive, like-minded women, start with one other woman and build from there.

☑ **Your Reminder** – Think of some of the most positive women who are pursuing their dreams. Consider what you can do to connect with them so that you can begin to cultivate your *You Go Girl* tribe.

➲ **Repeat This Aloud** – *Today I will reach out to other positive women and I will support and assist them as I seek their support.*

✎ **Journaling** - Reflect on the lessons learned from day 16 of the *Grab A Girlfriend and Go Live Your Dreams* 30-day challenge. Pick up a notepad or journal to be used exclusively for this 30-day program and write down at least one thing that you can do today to put the lessons learned from today's reading into practice. Use your journal to make any notes-to-self, journal your thoughts and feelings about today's task or jot down anything else that you feel prompted to write concerning your *Grab A Girlfriend and Go Live Your Dreams* journey.

Grab A Girlfriend and Go Live Your Dreams by Cassandra Mack

Day 17.
Own The Fact That You Are A Leader, A Creator and A Beautiful Dreamer

You wanna live well. *Right?* You wanna make more money than you've ever made before. *Right?* You wanna be known for your skills, gifts and talents. *Right?* You wanna go to bed each night feeling wonderful about who you are and what you're doing. *Right?* You want to know, that you know, that you know, that what you're doing matters and makes a difference? *Right?*

Well, the only way that these things are going to happen for you is if you own the fact that you are a LEADER, a CREATOR and a BEAUTIFUL DREAMER. You might not see yourself this way just yet. But it's true. You were born to lead. You were created to create. And you were destined to live out your beautiful dreams. Whether you lead and create in the kitchen, the classroom, the office, your garden, in your place of worship or right at home with your children or grandchildren, you are leading and creating all of the time. And you dream beautiful dreams all of the time.

The stuff that is INSIDE of you ...your gifts, talents, skills, dreams, ideas and the love you have to give: That's the stuff you have to get out there to the world! I don't care if you don't know how you're going to make it happen or if you tried something before and failed miserably, you were born to dream, lead and create. If you can dream up something in that beautiful mind of yours that you are truly inspired by and passionate about, you will naturally lead and create in that direction because that is who YOU truly are. And you will be successful!

Creative people are unconventional and eccentric. I know it. You know it. And everybody else knows it. We dance to our own beat and the music in our soul plays to its own key. That's it. There's something charming and irresistible about people like us, somehow we manage to see the world from a larger than life view, and the things we do, the choices we make are just different than what other people do.

Life it's not always easy for creative leaders like us. We may even fail at something a thousand times before we finally get it right. But we will rise and succeed in the end. If this sounds like you, then you need to own the fact that you are a LEADER, a CREATER and a BEAUTIFUL DREAMER. And that's all there is to it!

The beauty of owning who you are is that you can now show up for your life as your most Magnificent, Brilliant and Authentic self...with no apologies and no regrets. When you are 100% comfortable in your own skin, your dreams and goals become clearer to identify and easier to fulfill ...because You are no longer resisting. YOU are growing with the flow of life.

Here's an exercise: Make a list of no less than 12 things that make you creative, a leader and a beautiful dreamer. Keep this list handy so you can always own the fact that you are creative, a leader and a beautiful dreamer.

Here are 12 things that make me creative, a leader and a beautiful dreamer:

1. _____
2. _____
3. _____
4. _____
5. _____
6. _____
7. _____
8. _____
9. _____
10. _____
11. _____
12. _____

☑ **Your Reminder** – Think of some of the ways that you already create, lead and dream beautiful dreams. Consider what you can do to develop yourself even more as a creator, a leader and a beautiful dreamer.

➲ **Repeat This Aloud** – *Today I will own the fact that I am a leader, a creator and a beautiful dreamer.*

✐ **Journaling** - Reflect on the lessons learned from day 17 of the *Grab A Girlfriend and Go Live Your Dreams* 30-day challenge. Pick up a notepad or journal to be used exclusively for this 30-day program and write down at least one thing that you can do today to put the lessons learned from today's reading into practice. Use your journal to make any notes-

Grab A Girlfriend and Go Live Your Dreams by Cassandra Mack

to-self, journal your thoughts and feelings about today's task or jot down anything else that you feel prompted to write concerning your *Grab A Girlfriend and Go Live Your Dreams* journey.

Day 18.
Ask for What You Want & Clarify Your WHY

All my life I've been told that you can do anything that you set your mind to. But nobody tells you how to set your mind to doing the thing that you want to do. And there lies the problem. But there's also a real simple solution. It's this: *You have to ask for what you want, you've got to be specific and you've got to know your WHY.*

So here's what you're going to do today. Grab a pen and paper and write out exactly what you want from life. What does your dream life look like? You will probably start off vague and fuzzy, but I want you to stick with it and be as specific as possible. For example: If it's money that you want, identify exactly how much per month do you want to earn and WHY? If it's notoriety you want, identify exactly what's going to be your claim to fame and WHY? If you want to start your own business, what kind of business do you want to start and WHY?

Here's the other piece: Not only do you have to be specific about what you want, but you also have to know WHY you want it. Your WHY is the thing that gives your WHAT meaning.

So what this means for you is that you need to ask yourself if putting in the work to make your dreams come true would satisfy you on the soul level, because there has to be a deeper reason other than money, status or notoriety in order for you to feel fulfilled at the deepest level.

Grab A Girlfriend and Go Live Your Dreams by Cassandra Mack

This is one of the reasons why when people say that they want to pursue their dreams, they're unable to stick with it and go all in. Because they haven't identified their WHY. It's hard to stick with something and go all in if you don't know why you are doing what you're doing...you haven't attached a deeper meaning to your dream. You haven't identified your WHY.

The reason why I am doing what I love and living my life from my place of Magnificence, Brilliance and Authenticity is not because I know everything there is to know about the speaking, writing and coaching business or because I knew all of the right people; but because I finally got clear and specific about what I wanted and WHY. Then I gave myself permission to lead, dream and create, and I put in the work to bring my plans, dreams and ideas into fruition. And I am no different than you.

☑ **Your Reminder** – What do you really want? Ask for it today. Say it out loud and then expect to get it by putting in the work to make it happen. Don't forget to clarify your WHY.

⮑ **Repeat This Aloud** – *Today I will ask for what I want and I will identify my WHY.*

✏ **Journaling** - Reflect on the lessons learned from day 18 of the *Grab A Girlfriend and Go Live Your Dreams* 30-day challenge. Pick up a notepad or journal to be used exclusively for this 30-day program and write down at least one thing that you can do today to put the lessons learned from today's reading into practice. Use your journal to make any notes-to-self, journal your thoughts and feelings about today's task or jot down anything else that you feel prompted to write concerning your *Grab A Girlfriend and Go Live Your Dreams* journey.

Day 19.
Can You Withstand The Pain?

One of my favorite places to go to in the spring is the Botanical Gardens in Brooklyn, New York. It's one of the places that my mom used to take me when I was a little girl. I use to love to walk past the rose garden and marvel at the beauty and splendor of the roses. Roses are beautiful. They smell absolutely divine. And believe it or not, for many insects roses are sweet to taste. But as beautiful and splendid as roses are, you can't have the rose without the thorn.

Did you know that the reason why rose plants grow thorns is to prevent insects from eating them? Thorns are the only way that roses have to protect themselves from being destroyed by insects who likes how they taste. Thorns are nature's way of protecting the rose and making sure that they come into full bloom. Because without the thorns, the roses would not last very long and we as humans would not be able to enjoy their beauty. So, a rose plant's thorns are nature's way of keeping roses from being eaten alive.

For many, who do not understand that nature's intended purpose for the rose is to grow from a mustard-sized seed into a flower that comes into full bloom. And to add beauty to the world rather than for us to prematurely pick the rose while it is still growing or put it in a vase for our decor until it slowly dies. It seems odd that a flower which is so beautiful to the eye can also be

Grab A Girlfriend and Go Live Your Dreams by Cassandra Mack

the source of so much pain if we prick our finger on one of its thorns.

So in essence, thorns are annoying, bothersome and frustrating. And depending on the size and serration of the thorn, it can feel like the thorn was created solely to serve as a prick. But nothing could be further from the truth. Because once again you cannot enjoy the beauty of the rose without understanding the purpose of the thorn.

Did you know that our dreams are like that bed of roses and our blood, sweat and tears are like the thorns? So my question for you is: What pain are you willing to endure in order to smell your roses? Whether you want to sell a million books, make a million dollars, or change a million lives, any dream worth having is a dream worth pricking your finger for. Not only that, the bigger the thing that you are giving birth to, the greater the labor pains. After all you can't build your mental, emotional and spiritual endurance without going through labor. Fitness experts understand this concept in terms of lifting weights. The reason a personal trainer trains people to push through the pain of exercise by lifting weights is so their muscles can be strengthened and they can build endurance. Not only that, a good personal trainer will make you do repetitions – meaning you will have to repeat the process of lifting weights even if it hurts until you start to build your strength.

The biggest pipe dream that we were ever sold was that living our dreams would be easy. This is simply not true. In fact, as you pursue your dreams, you will be tested beyond measure,

Grab A Girlfriend and Go Live Your Dreams by Cassandra Mack

tried to the breaking point and you will get your feelings hurt. Yet and still, you have to push through the pain and build your endurance. You have to endure the pain in order to give birth. So it's not a matter of if you are going to experience pain, it's a matter of WHEN and how much you're willing to endure. It's a matter of pushing through the pain of disappointment, setbacks and rejection and getting back up each and every time life knocks you down. Because the reality of being in it to win it is this: Champions stay in the ring.

So today, my question for you is: *What are you willing to endure in order to give birth to your dreams? When the labor pains of life become intense will you cave in to the pressure or will you push through it until you give birth?*

In the space below, write down at least three things that you've got going for you that give you the strength to endure.

I have the strength to endure because ....

_____

_____

_____

_____

_____

_____

_____

_____

_____

_____

_____

_____

_____

Grab A Girlfriend and Go Live Your Dreams by Cassandra Mack

☑ **Your Reminder** – Consider what you need to do differently in order to build up your endurance, so that you can give birth to your labor of love. Make a commitment to build up your tolerance for the labor pains of life.

↻ **Repeat This Aloud** – *I am willing to go through the labor pains so that I can deliver the life of my dreams.*

✎ **Journaling** - Reflect on the lessons learned from day 19 of the *Grab A Girlfriend and Go Live Your Dreams* 30-day challenge. Pick up a notepad or journal to be used exclusively for this 30-day program and write down at least one thing that you can do today to put the lessons learned from today's reading into practice. Use your journal to make any notes-to-self, journal your thoughts and feelings about today's task or jot down anything else that you feel prompted to write concerning your *Grab A Girlfriend and Go Live Your Dreams* journey.

Day 20.
Get Into S.D.M
Success. Driven. Mode.

When you consider all that you want to do with your life, do you really think you're being as productive as you could be? *Be honest.* When you think about how you allow the hours to pass you by and all of the things that need to get done as well as all of the plans that you say you want to accomplish...are you being as productive as you could be? When you think about what your life could look like if you gave it your all, can you honestly say that you're handling your business in the most effective and fruitful way?

Speaking for myself, there are days when I am totally on my *A-Game*, but then there are also days when I look at how I spend my time, how the week has flown by, how my life still has a lot of areas that need pruning and fine-tuning ....and I wonder *when am I going to get my ish together.*

Have you ever felt this way?

Whenever I find myself procrastinating to the point of falling into a rut and cruising on SNOOZE control, so to speak, I know it's time for me to get off my butt and get into S.D.M. otherwise known as *Success Driven Mode.*

If you feel like you need to step it up and get into S.D.M. here are 5 tips to help you.

1.) **Go Harder** – If you've ever had a really intense workout at the gym, you know what it means to go hard or go home. When you go harder at your workout; you already know that you're

Grab A Girlfriend and Go Live Your Dreams by Cassandra Mack

going to sweat profusely, your body is going to hurt like crazy and everything inside of you feels like it's going to kill over. *Right*? However, after the work-out you feel an enormous sense of accomplishment, because you pushed yourself and did the darn thing. You need to apply this same concept to living your dreams. Whatever you are doing to move your life in the direction of your dreams, go even harder. If you are working on a book and writing 1 page a day, go harder and push yourself to write 3 pages a day. If you are trying to drum up sales for your business and you're reaching out to 3 prospects a day, go harder and reach out to 5 prospects a day.

2.) **Now Is The Time** – Stop waiting for your life to be perfect. The time to move your life in the direction of your dreams is now, not when you lose 20 lbs, get yourself together, have the perfect business plan or any other excuse you've made to delay your dreams. Start now. Your life is now. Press play and start.

3.) **Work On Your Dreams In Between The Cracks and Crevices of Life** – Want to know when I conceived most of the ideas for my creative ventures and books? While waiting in the doctor's office, my travel time on the subway, early mornings before I woke my son up for school, late nights when I could not fall back to sleep, sitting in the playground while my son was playing with his friends, sipping on a cup of coffee at Dunkin Donuts. Do you see where I'm going with this? When you feel

Grab A Girlfriend and Go Live Your Dreams by Cassandra Mack

like you don't have the time because your schedule is extremely inundated, then you can work on your dreams in between the cracks and crevices of your life. When you find the time to do the things that excite your soul, you begin to manifest your dreams a little bit more each day.

4.) **Be Extremely Protective of Your Time** – You only get 24 hours in a day and you spend at least 6 to 8 hours of that time sleeping. This means that you've got to have your priorities in order and learn to become protective of your time. Time is the commodity of your life and if you allow people to get you sucked up into their drama or things that have nothing to do with you, then you won't have the time to invest in the building of your dreams. Don't be afraid to be protective of your time so that you can invest it in the things that are most important to you.

5.) **Stick To The Basics** – Eat right. Move your body. Drink lots of water. Get enough rest. Say something encouraging to yourself to pump you up for the day. Give thanks and praise and then ask God for guidance. Do something daily that moves you one step closer to your goals and over time you'll see progress. That's it. These are the basics. Make sure that you are doing the basics to get your mind, body and emotions into success driven mode.

Grab A Girlfriend and Go Live Your Dreams by Cassandra Mack

Getting into S.D.M. *Success Driven Mode* is really about being proactive and productive, even when you don't feel like it, even when you're feeling discouraged and disappointed, even when you rather lay in bed and be lazy, even when you don't know what to do or how you're doing to do it. You've got to decide, right now that you are going to go all in and get into *Success Driven Mode.* Today is the day to gear up and get into *Success Driven Mode.*

☑ **Your Reminder** – Make up your mind to get into *Success Driven Mode* today. Be prepared to do the grunt work of your dreams. Start now.

➲ **Repeat This Aloud** – *I am gearing myself up to get into Success Driven Mode.*

✎ **Journaling** - Reflect on the lessons learned from day 20 of the *Grab A Girlfriend and Go Live Your Dreams* 30-day challenge. Pick up a notepad or journal to be used exclusively for this 30-day program and write down at least one thing that you can do today to put the lessons learned from today's reading into practice. Use your journal to make any notes-to-self, journal your thoughts and feelings about today's task or jot down anything else that you feel prompted to write concerning your *Grab A Girlfriend and Go Live Your Dreams* journey.

Self Check-In

✓ What have you accomplished thus far, since doing the *Grab A Girlfriend and Go Live Your Dreams* 30 day challenge? *(either big or small)*

✓ How do you feel right now about the progress you've made thus far?

✓ Was there any part of the program that you were struggling to follow-thru on? If yes, why were you struggling with that particular part of the challenge?

✓ Write down one thing that you can do this week to move your life one step closer to living your dreams.

Girlfriend Check-In

Now we've come to the girlfriend check-in. This is your time to discuss your successes and challenges regarding your journey thus far. Remember that this is an important part of your progress because it enables you to process the work that you've done throughout each 10-day module with your accountability partner. You should have a pen and notebook handy so that you can jot down any helpful ideas or suggestions that come out of your girlfriend check-in.

Summarize 3 things that you did this week to move your life in the direction that you want it to go in. Talk about any challenges you have faced. Ask for feedback. Do not argue with your accountability partner. Simply thank her for listening and jot down anything that is helpful and useful.

_____

_____

_____

_____

_____

_____

_____

_____

_____

_____

Grab A Girlfriend and Go Live Your Dreams by Cassandra Mack

Dream Work Check List

1. Give Voice to Your Dream.

2. Put Your Past In Its Place.

3. Adjust Your Spending To Support Your Dreams.

4. Feed Your Dreams With Mini Goals.

5. Don't Cater To Your Haters.

6. Cultivate Your Very Own ...You Go Girl! Tribe.

7. Own The Fact That You Are A Leader, A Creator and A Beautiful Dreamer.

8. Ask for What You Want and Clarify Your WHY.

9. Develop The Mental Muscles to Withstand The Labor Pains of Your Dream.

10. Get Into S.D.M. Success Driven Mode.

Grab A Girlfriend and Go Live Your Dreams by Cassandra Mack

Part 3.
Do It

Grab A Girlfriend and Go Live Your Dreams by Cassandra Mack

Day 21.
Create Daily Success Routines

The road to success is simple. You're either going to put in the work to make it happen or you are not. Whatever your definition of success is, whatever your vision is for your life, you either want it bad enough to create daily routines to make it happen or you don't. So if you want to be successful as defined by you, you've got to create daily a routine that will enable you to drive the results that you are seeking.

If your daily routine consists of productive habits intended to get you closer to your dreams, you will come to a place where you are doing what you are passionate about and earning the kind of income that enables you to live out your definition of success. Below are 10 habits that you should consider incorporating into your daily success routine.

1.) **Spend The First Hour of Your Day Planning, Praying and Visualizing.** – Before you turn on your computer, or the TV or get on the phone, spend the first hour of the day getting clear and centered. If you cannot spend an hour then do 30-minutes or 15-miuntes. The point is when you give the first part of your day to God, you start your day off clearer, more focused, and intentional.

2.) **Begin Your Day Early** - Successful people wake up early. Because the earlier that you begin your day, the more time you'll have to

Grab A Girlfriend and Go Live Your Dreams by Cassandra Mack

accomplish your plans and tasks. When you wake up early, you're better prepared to face the day ready for whatever comes your way because you've given yourself the additional time to manifest your plans and make adjustments as needed.

3.) Plan For The Next Day The Night Before – Planning out your priorities the night before enables you to focus your time, energy and resources on what's important, what needs to be done first and what else you need to complete in order to get achieve your goals for the day.

4.) Keep Your Goals By Your Bedside- I write my goals down on index cards and keep them on a little table by my bedside. This way when I get up, I can see what needs to get done and I can start my day off focused on my primary priorities.

5.) Drink More Water and Get Some Sort of Exercise – You have to take care of your body if you want to have the energy and vitality to pursue your dreams. Drinking plenty of water and incorporating regular exercise into your regimen will keep your body healthy and strong.

6.) Ask Yourself: What Are The 3 Most Important Things That I Must Get Done Today? Asking yourself this question enables you to work on your plans in their order of importance so that you accomplish the most important tasks first.

7.) View Success With The Right Attitude - This habit is all about knowing what matters most in life and acknowledging the areas in your life where you are already successful. If you really want to live a successful life, you must acknowledge the areas in your life where you are already succeeding and then use this positive mindset to motivate you in the other areas of your life. This tip is all about counting your blessings.

8.) Invest More of Your Income On Things That Will Grow Your Dream – There's nothing wrong with spending money every once in a while on pampering yourself or entertainment. However, the majority of your income after bills are paid and money is put away for your nest egg, should be spent on growing yourself, your business or your dream. Don't spend your money on things to impress people. Invest it in things that grow you, better your life, create a nest egg and propel you closer to your dream.

9.) Write Your Dreams Down On A White Board or Poster Board – Having your dreams in big letters in front of you keeps your dreams in the forefront of your mind. Having your dreams on a white board where you can see them daily serves as a reminder of why you are doing what you're doing. You can also create a vision board, where you place pictures of your

Grab A Girlfriend and Go Live Your Dreams by Cassandra Mack

aspirations, goals and dreams on a poster board.

10.) Your Family Comes First – Your loved ones come first. If you have a spouse and children, then your family is your first priority because you are going to require their love, support and understanding. Share your dreams with your family. Discuss how your dreams can be incorporated into your family's vision and how your dreams can bring greater blessings to your family.

☑ **Your Reminder** – Take some time to find the answer to this question: *What should I be doing more of or less of, so that I can put some daily success routines in place?*

⟳ **Repeat This Aloud** – *I have the discipline to create a daily success routine.*

✎ **Journaling** - Reflect on the lessons learned from day 21 of the *Grab A Girlfriend and Go Live Your Dreams* 30-day challenge. Pick up a notepad or journal to be used exclusively for this 30-day program and write down at least one thing that you can do today to put the lessons learned from today's reading into practice. Use your journal to make any notes-to-self, journal your thoughts and feelings about today's task or jot down anything else that you feel prompted to write concerning your *Grab A Girlfriend and Go Live Your Dreams* journey.

Day 22.
Think On Paper

One of the most effective strategies for achieving all of your life's ambitions is to think on paper. It's important to set goals that inspire you to grow personally and professionally. But it's even more important to write your goals down. Writing your goals down, forces your subconscious mind to keep a mental record of your future plans and dreams.

Your ultimate success relies on having and achieving concrete measurable goals. Thinking on paper allows you to do two things: 1.) figure out whether you are directing your time and energy in the right direction 2.) Track your progress.

No matter how you cut it, goals are necessary. Goals help you get from where you are now to where you want to be.

Experts in the psychology of achievement say that your goals should be as specific and measurable as possible so that your subconscious mind can mentally store the information for future reference and hone in on the experiences and opportunities that will help you get where you are trying to go.

For example: If you have a goal of losing weight, write this goal down but, instead of writing, *My goal is to lose weight.* Write it down in measurable terms, such as: *I will lose five pounds by next month.* You can also expand on your goal by writing down how you plan achieve it. *I will lose five pounds by next month by exercising for 30*

Grab A Girlfriend and Go Live Your Dreams by Cassandra Mack

minutes each day and eating a well-balanced diet that is low in fat and refined sugars.

When you write down your goals, don't be afraid to set goals that stretch you. If you are going to take your life to the next level, then you've got to enlarge your vision of what's possible for you.

With this idea in mind, here is a 9-step process to help you think on paper and clarify your goals.

Step. 1 Decide What You Want To Achieve, Accomplish and Contribute.

Set goals for every area of your life. Decide what you want to achieve, accomplish and contribute in every area of your life both personally and professionally. Give some serious thought to what you want for yourself in each of these areas. Write your answers down.

Step. 2 Set A Deadline.

The subconscious mind responds to dates and deadlines. The more specific the deadline, the more likely you'll be to hit your intended target. Think of a deadline as an estimated completion date based on your current skills, knowledge and resources. If you don't reach your goal by the estimated deadline, take inventory of your skills and resources then adjust your deadline.

Grab A Girlfriend and Go Live Your Dreams by Cassandra Mack

Step. 3 Identify Potential Obstacles and Challenges.

Consider some of the potential obstacles and challenges that might interfere with your goals. Identify the things that are going on inside of you or around you that may create interference or cause a barrier in some way. For every obstacle that you've identified, write down a plan to overcome or work around it.

Step 4 Identify The Knowledge, Skills and Personal Traits Needed To Achieve Your Goals

If you are going to achieve something you've never achieved before, you are going to have to learn, do and become something you've never been before. Identify the things in your life that you need to work on. Pick, one thing and start working on it.

Step. 5 Identify The People, Groups and Organizations That Can Help You Achieve Your Goals.

Who do you know that can help you the most? What can you offer in return to make it a win/win situation? Perhaps you know someone who has the skills to fine-tune your resume and you'd like their input, what can you offer in return? Write this down.

Step 6. *Organize Your Goals By Priority*

Start with the goal that will have the greatest impact on all of your other goals. Is there one goal that will help you accomplish all of your other plans faster? If the answer is yes, then that goal should be your #1 priority where you put the majority of your time, energy and resources into. Organize all of your other goals around your primary goal. To do this, you need to know: Which goals need to be completed first and by when? Are there any goals that are dependent upon you accomplishing another goal in a different area?

Step 7. *Do Something Each Day That Moves You In The Direction of Your Goals.*

Every day, no matter how small, do something that moves you in the direction of your goals. Don't let procrastination and complacency set in. Set a regularly scheduled time to do at least one thing that will aide you in the achievement of your plans. Read an article, make a cold call, practice a skill. They key is to get in the habit of doing something each day that moves you in the direction of your goals.

Grab A Girlfriend and Go Live Your Dreams by Cassandra Mack

Step 8. Visualize Yourself Achieving Your Goals.

See yourself achieving your goals. Let yourself feel the feelings that come with the achievement of your desired goal. Dig deep within and emotionally experience the feelings of excitement, joy, satisfaction and confidence as you achieve your goals. See yourself vividly. Better yet, get yourself some poster board and make a vision board consisting of pictures, words and images that capture the essence of your plans and dreams.

Step 9. Develop An Obsession For Winning.

It's been said that the authors of the Chicken Soup for The Soul Series, sent their first book out to 144 publishers and got rejected be each and every one of them. However, no matter how many rejection letters they received, they kept sending out their manuscript until one day, a publisher signed them and now they rest is history. The authors now sit on a multi-million dollar publishing empire and are reaping the rewards of their persistence.

It's important for you to believe in yourself even if no one else believes in you. Sometimes other people are just too narrow-minded in their thinking to see your vision. Don't allow someone else's short-sightedness to cause you to cut your

Grab A Girlfriend and Go Live Your Dreams by Cassandra Mack

dreams short. You just never know when your breakthrough is going to come. Never give up on yourself. No matter what obstacles come your way, always remember that he who stays in the race eventually crosses the finish line.

☑ **Your Reminder** – Think on paper. What good ideas do you have lurking in the back of your mind that you need to write down? Get yourself a notebook and write them down.

➲ **Repeat This Aloud** – *Today I will think on paper. As soon as I have a good idea I will write it down.*

✎ **Journaling** - Reflect on the lessons learned from day 22 of the *Grab A Girlfriend and Go Live Your Dreams* 30-day challenge. Pick up a notepad or journal to be used exclusively for this 30-day program and write down at least one thing that you can do today to put the lessons learned from today's reading into practice. Use your journal to make any notes-to-self, journal your thoughts and feelings about today's task or jot down anything else that you feel prompted to write concerning your *Grab A Girlfriend and Go Live Your Dreams* journey.

Day 23.
Let Your Highest Values Serve As Your Guideposts

Values guide every decision you make therefore directing your destiny. If you want to live your dreams and achieve the deepest level of success as defined by you, you have to know what your highest values are and let them serve as your guide for how you walk through life.

Why? Because if you are not clear about what's most important to you and what you truly stand for, you may find yourself getting sidetracked rather than decisively determining the best course of action to catapult your dreams.

It goes without saying that your values are the foundation for your life because everything you do and pursue is built around what you value most. Your life is the sum total of you decisions, which are based on your values. So if you find that you're having a tough time making or sticking to a decision, it's usually an indication that you are not clear about what you value most in that particular situation.

When you know what your values are, decision-making becomes a whole lot easier, because your decisions will be based on your highest ideals.

Take some time to clarify your values. In order to figure out what your values are, ask yourself: "What's most important to me at this point in my life?" Is it peace of mind? Happiness? Health? Family? Money? Being a good person?

Giving back to the community? Leaving a powerful legacy?

Write your values down in their order of importance, starting with the most important one and ending with the least.

_____

_____

_____

_____

_____

_____

_____

_____

When you have finished, review your values and assess whether or not your values are helping you to achieve your desired life or hindering you. If a value is hindering you from living your desired life, reevaluate that value. Then, adjust your values accordingly.

Sometimes it can be difficult to get a clear picture of your highest values, because we are so inundated with media messages that seek to sell us on what's important. But, only you can decide which values are important to you. You and you alone determine your values. Always remember that your values, whatever they might be, are the motivating force that creates your life's path. Following are some questions designed to get you thinking about your values.

- If a good year blimp were to fly across the sky with a banner describing three things that you stand for, what would it say?

Grab A Girlfriend and Go Live Your Dreams by Cassandra Mack

- If you could spend one day with any person who ever lived who would it be and why?
- If you could have one prayer answered, what would it be and why?
- Describe a time when you felt real strong about a cause or issue. What do you think this says about your highest values?
- Your high school newspaper tracked you down and asked if they could do a story on you, what would you want the headline of your story to be? What would you want the body of the article to say about you? What do your answers tell you about your values?
- If you could solve one problem for the world what would it be and why?

Your answers to these questions should give you additional insight into your highest values. With this idea in mind, ask yourself: *Are there any changes that I need to make in my life so that I can allow my highest values to serve as my guidepost?*

☑ **Your Reminder** – Remember _ your life is the sum total of your values. So get in the habit of evaluating your values to make sure that your highest values are driving your life.

⟳ **Repeat This Aloud** – *Today I will live by my highest values.*

🖉 **Journaling** - Reflect on the lessons learned from day 23 of the *Grab A Girlfriend and Go Live Your Dreams* 30-day challenge. Pick up a notepad or journal to be used exclusively for this 30-day program and write down at least one thing that you can do today to put the lessons learned from today's reading into practice. Use your journal to make any notes-to-self, journal your thoughts and feelings about today's task or jot down anything else that you feel prompted to write concerning your *Grab A Girlfriend and Go Live Your Dreams* journey.

Day 24.
Remember That Every Step Counts

The only way to create something incredible is to persistently pursue it. So here's the hard, cold truth about living your dreams: If you're not prepared to be relentless about making your dreams a reality, if you're not prepared to keep on keeping on even when life gets, complicated and crazy and if you're not prepared to do like the *Energizer Bunny* commercial and "take a licking and keep on ticking," then you are not prepared to live your dreams. Because every step you take counts in the grand scheme of your dreams. Every step you take in the direction of your dreams leads you one step closer to living the life that you envision. So today we are stressing the importance of ...Recognizing that every step counts.

For years successful men and women have understood the phrase: *Every step counts.* These three simple words pack a lot of power, because every step that you take in the direction of your goals has an accumulative effect towards your dreams. The longer you work at your goals and the more effort you put into the things you want out of life, the greater your chances of accomplishing your goals. The problem with most people is not that they don't have the skill or talent. It's that they don't have staying power. They give up too quickly and throw in the towel at the first sign of difficulty.

Grab A Girlfriend and Go Live Your Dreams by Cassandra Mack

Every effort that you make towards the things you want in life is like making a deposit in your success account. Over time no matter how small your efforts, your account will begin to pay interest in the form of a completed task, or an accomplished goal.

Your progress in life is directly related to how much sustained effort you put into your dreams. If you read or watch any biography of any successful person, even the people who appear to be an overnight success, you will find that they stayed the course no matter how many obstacles came their way. Even more, they did something on a regular basis to move themselves closer to their goals and dreams. Here's the biggest part, whenever they were knocked down, they dusted themselves off and got back up.

On a daily basis you should ask yourself this question: *What can I do today to get one step closer to my dreams?* Take five minutes right now to make a mental note of one small thing that you can do today to get one step closer to your dreams. Learn to practice sustained effort so that you can keep pushing...no matter what.

☑ **Your Reminder** – Work to increase your momentum. Develop the characteristic of persistence.

⟳ **Repeat This Aloud** – *Today I will take another step in the direction of my dreams.*

✎ **Journaling** - Reflect on the lessons learned from day 24 of the *Grab A Girlfriend and Go*

Grab A Girlfriend and Go Live Your Dreams by Cassandra Mack

Live Your Dreams 30-day challenge. Pick up a notepad or journal to be used exclusively for this 30-day program and write down at least one thing that you can do today to put the lessons learned from today's reading into practice. Use your journal to make any notes-to-self, journal your thoughts and feelings about today's task or jot down anything else that you feel prompted to write concerning your *Grab A Girlfriend and Go Live Your Dreams* journey.

Day 25.
Let Go of Habits
That Do Not Serve You Well

We all have habits that either hinder us or help us. The key to reaching your goals faster is learning to let go of habits that do not serve you well and that are not in alignment with what you are seeking to achieve. Reason being is, it's going to be pretty difficult to live your dreams if you have habits that are not allowing you to be your best and brightest self. Sure you can pursue your dreams while holding on to bad habits. But by doing so, you slow down your rate of progress. This is why it's important to practice the strategy of **ASSESS and LET GO!**

This strategy is all about assessing whether or not a particular habit is helping you get closer to your dreams and then letting go of the habits that are not serving you well.

Here's why it is so critical to let go of habits that do not serve you well. If you engage in a behavior long enough, over time it becomes a habit. And the trouble with habits is that we do them without thinking about what we are doing. And whenever we are not thinking about what we are doing, we cannot see the harmful effects of a particular choice or action. For example, if you have a habit of eating junk food late at night, you're probably not thinking about how this choice is affecting your overall health and level of energy. This is why it is so important that you pay

Grab A Girlfriend and Go Live Your Dreams by Cassandra Mack

attention to your habits, especially the ones that do not serve you well.

So my question for you is: *Are your habits serving you well?* If not, it might be well worth the effort to make a few changes. Start by taking an inventory of your habits. Identify the ones that are undesirable or counterproductive. Then summon up the willpower to stop doing them.

Bad habits can be your worst enemy, especially if they get in the way of your health, happiness, rate of success or peace of mind. Almost everything we do is a result of habit, from our morning routine, to what we eat, to the way we dress, to what we do with our leisure time.

The most powerful way to rid yourself of a bad habit is to adopt a new behavior that is more in line with how you want to feel and where you want to take your life. Today, set your mind to assessing your habits and letting go of those that are not in alignment with where you want to take your life. Adopt the attitude that nothing will stand in your way, and that you have the power to cast aside any habits that are not consistent with the type of person you want to become and the life you want to live.

☑ **Your Reminder** – Some bad habits are more obvious than others like: smoking, overspending and overeating. Then there are those habits that are not as easy to recognize because they are so deeply ingrained in our behavior patterns that they become our blind spots like: constantly letting people take advantage of you then getting upset because you feel like you've been used, allowing fear to

Grab A Girlfriend and Go Live Your Dreams by Cassandra Mack

hold you back or continually getting into relationship with people who are not good for you. Today take a little time to give some serious thought to the less obvious habits that might be holding you back.

☑ **Repeat This Aloud** – *Today I am letting go of habits that do not serve me well.*

✎ **Journaling** - Reflect on the lessons learned from day 25 of the *Grab A Girlfriend and Go Live Your Dreams* 30-day challenge. Pick up a notepad or journal to be used exclusively for this 30-day program and write down at least one thing that you can do today to put the lessons learned from today's reading into practice. Use your journal to make any notes-to-self, journal your thoughts and feelings about today's task or jot down anything else that you feel prompted to write concerning your *Grab A Girlfriend and Go Live Your Dreams* journey.

Day 26.
Be Willing To Wash
A Few Backs

Ever heard the saying: *You wash my back, and I'll wash yours?* Well it's true, because the quickest way to get support for your plans and dreams is to support other people with theirs first. Always remember the golden rule of life: *You don't get something for nothing.* In essence, treat people well and give of yourself first before asking for support. Most people enter into relationships trying to figure out what other people can do for them instead of applying the *Wash A Few Backs* philosophy and then wonder why they can't get anyone to support them with their endeavors.

This is the wrong approach because when you come at people from a position of always having your hand out instead of sometimes having your hand up to lift someone else, you come across as a self-seeking individual. People who want to live prosperously understand that when you sow into the lives of others, you create a cycle of reciprocity in which other people will sow back into your life.

Be a giver rather than a taker by making positive relationship deposits in the lives of the other people. Instead of always asking: What's in it for me? Ask yourself: How can I become a greater blessing to others? As a result of you paying it forwarded, the support that you are seeking will boomerang back to you.

Be good to people wherever you go because you never know how one little random act of kindness can brighten someone's day. Imagine what the world would be like if everyone decided to treat each other well. Our communities would be safer. Our children would grow up feeling nurtured and encouraged. Our jobs would become more fulfilling and we would be happier, healthier and more productive citizens.

The other part about developing mutually supportive relationships is when you do so, you accelerate the pace at which you reach your own goals. And you never know when you may need to call on some of those relationships. People may not remember your name, your pedigree or what you do for a living, but they will always remember how you treated them.

Today do a mental walk through of all the people whom you know who can help you accelerate your path to success, and then ask yourself: *What can I do to develop more mutually beneficial relationships with them?*

☑ **Your Reminder** – Make sure that you approach your relationships from a position of reciprocity. What can you do to develop more mutually beneficial relationships?

⊃ **Repeat This Aloud** – *Today I will go out of my way to treat people well and look for ways to add value to my relationships.*

✎ **Journaling** - Reflect on the lessons learned from day 26 of the *Grab A Girlfriend and Go*

Live Your Dreams 30-day challenge. Pick up a notepad or journal to be used exclusively for this 30-day program and write down at least one thing that you can do today to put the lessons learned from today's reading into practice. Use your journal to make any notes-to-self, journal your thoughts and feelings about today's task or jot down anything else that you feel prompted to write concerning your *Grab A Girlfriend and Go Live Your Dreams* journey.

Day 27.
Get The Inside Scoop On Your Dreams

Ever got the inside scoop on a great shoe sale or a hot, new restaurant's grand opening? If the answer is yes, then you already know that whenever you get the inside scoop on something, what you're actually getting is first-hand information that is exclusively reserved for insiders and exceptional customers. And this enables you to get more bang for your buck and stay one step ahead of the game with respect to the thing you're getting the inside scoop on. Did you know that this same approach works well when it comes to living your dreams?

You see, dreams come in all shapes and sizes. Not only that, your dreams are often much more attainable than you think. However, one of the quickest ways to speed up the process of getting there is to get the inside scoop on your dreams, by talking to people who are where you want to be.

A key aspect of following your dreams involves not only deciding what you want to do with your life, but also researching your dream in order to develop a better understanding of the steps you'll need to take to get from point A to B.

By getting the inside scoop, you'll be more knowledgeable about all of the options that are available to you. Plus, you'll get insider info on what you need to tweak in order to double your productivity and accelerate your path to success.

Grab A Girlfriend and Go Live Your Dreams by Cassandra Mack

Here are some ways that you can get the inside scoop on your dreams:

1.) Consider a short-term work experience in the industry.
2.) Volunteer to assist one of your mentors with a project that he or she is working on.
3.) Invest in a couple of coaching sessions with a life coach who is already doing what you want to do.

The good thing about getting the inside scope on your dreams is you'll have the opportunity to test the waters to make sure that the dream you've been imagining inside your head is one that you want to actually pursue once you realize the amount of work it will take to get there.

☑ **Your Reminder** – Pay attention to the hustle that's attached to your dream so that you can figure out if this particular dream is something you want to pursue right now or if you want to shift gears and put your energy in a different direction.

⟳ **Repeat This Aloud** – *Today I am going to get the inside scoop on my dream. My dream is attainable and once I find out exactly what achieving my dream entails, I can take the necessary steps to make my dream a reality.*

🖊 **Journaling** - Reflect on the lessons learned from day 27 of the *Grab A Girlfriend and Go Live Your Dreams* 30-day challenge. Pick up a notepad or journal to be used exclusively for this 30-day program and write down at least one thing that you can do today to put the lessons learned from today's reading into practice. Use your journal to make any notes-to-self, journal your thoughts and feelings about today's task or jot down anything else that you feel prompted to write concerning your *Grab A Girlfriend and Go Live Your Dreams* journey.

Day 28.

Date Yourself Like You Would Date An Individual Who You Were Super Excited About

Have you ever got all dressed up and taken yourself out on a date? To your favorite restaurant, musical, book signing or museum? I have. As crazy as it sounds, taking yourself on a date is good for your self-esteem. Why? Because, dating yourself teaches you these 3 things, how to: rely on yourself when no one else comes through for you, show up boldly for your life and it keeps your passions in front of you.

Taking yourself on a date teaches you how to enjoy your own company, rediscover your passions and most of all it reinforces the importance of treating yourself special. A lot of women forget to nurture themselves as they juggle the competing demands on their time, but it's important for you to take the time to fall in love with your life so that your dreams never die.

Let's use dating a man as an analogy for dating yourself. Suppose for a moment that you were looking to meet your Mr. Right. Where would you start? Well for starters, you would probably put yourself out there and go out on dates. That's the only way that you're going to increase the likelihood of meeting your Mr. Right. Dating provides you with an opportunity to get to know other people. Dating gives you a chance to figure out if your personalities, goals, and values are compatible. Dating allows you to learn about a potential partner's likes, dislikes, background, passions, beliefs, and everything else you need to know in order to assess if you have enough in common with a guy to give it a try.

Having this knowledge about a potential partner is a crucial step in getting to know a person and figuring out if you want to take things any further. Believe it or not, your dreams work in the exact same way. The only way you're going to know if there's enough chemistry and compatibility with a particular dream is to spend some time with it. This way you'll have enough information to decide if the dream that you say you really, really want to pursue is the right one for you.

Imagine getting acquainted with your dreams and passions on a deeper level. Can you imagine what your life would look like if you treated your secret longings and heartfelt desires with the same kind of attentiveness, respect and care that you would give to a guy you really, really like? Well, the best way to rediscover your passions and fall in love with your life is to date yourself like you would date a man who you were super excited about. If you've never dated yourself, here are 5 tips to help you ease into it.

1. **Choose A Place To Go** – Now this may seem obvious, but if you were to date yourself, where would you take YOU? For example if you have a dream of selling your handmade jewelry on the internet, a great date night for you might be to take yourself on a date to a craft show or a street fair where handmade jewelry is sold.

Grab A Girlfriend and Go Live Your Dreams by Cassandra Mack

2. **Wear Something Special** – If you were going on a date with a guy who you were interested in and who you wanted to make a great first impression on, wouldn't you put some effort into your appearance? Well aren't you interested in getting to know you and getting reacquainted with your dreams? For example, when I took myself to the Opera last year, I wore a little black dress with a strand of pearls and a pair of leopard stilettos with a matching leopard handbag. I looked fabulous. And I felt fabulous. It was important for me to feel special, look special and treat myself special for this very special evening that I would be spending ~~by~~ ...I mean WITH myself

3. **Have A Plan** - What are you going to do once you get to your chosen location? For example, if you were going to a craft fair to check out handmade jewelry, perhaps you could plan to bring cards with pictures of your handmade jewelry or you could wear one of your pieces and plan to introduce yourself to at least two vendors at the craft fair.

4. **Give Yourself A Thoughtful Gift** – Anything from fragrant body lotion to flowers, or a note that you write to yourself and place in a gift box. Giving yourself a gift on your date night signifies that you are going to give yourself the love, nurturance and special attention that you deserve. When I took myself on my date to the Opera, not only did I dress up, I bought myself some fresh flowers and a mini box of

Grab A Girlfriend and Go Live Your Dreams by Cassandra Mack

Godiva Chocolate to signify how special my evening was going to be and to celebrate how good I wanted to feel about me.

5. **Get Excited** – You know how you get excited when you're looking forward to going on a date with someone who you are interested in and excited about? Well, summon up that same excitement and apply it to yourself. After all, you are going on a date with someone very special...YOU.

By dating yourself, you accomplish three major things: First, you learn to treat yourself the way you want other people to treat you. Second, you delve deeper into the things that peak your interests and intrigue you. And third, you will no longer be afraid of taking risks and trying new things because you conquered that fear when you went out solo.

Use your *Date Time* to do all the things that you've always wanted to do, but pushed aside to accommodate other people or because you couldn't get anyone else to go with you.

Cherish the special moments that you get to spend with the one person who will always know what it feels like to be YOU. And if you think that dating yourself is narcissistic, it's not. It's about self-pampering and self-care. If you don't believe me, think about all the times you felt alone. Now think of all the times you felt like you were on top of the world. What is the common denominator in both of these scenarios? It's YOU! You are the

Grab A Girlfriend and Go Live Your Dreams by Cassandra Mack

common denominator in your life. Therefore, you must take good care of you.

There is only one person in this great big world who has experienced every minute of your life with you. And that's YOU! You were the one person who was there for you, even when other people let you down or simply could not be what you needed them to be. But YOU can always be who and what YOU need YOU to be.

You and you alone, are the only one who has battled your inner demons and kept your deepest secrets that not even your very best friend knows. You are the only one who understands the pain, the joy and the struggles that you've been through. You are the only one who has felt the kind of disappointment that comes from feeling stuck, trapped and so discouraged that you can't even put your feelings into words. You've seen yourself at your worst, and you've been with you at your best.

So this is WHY, you must absolutely date yourself with the same level of intensity, passion, care, attentiveness, enthusiasm and effort that you would date a man who you were super excited about. Because at the end of the day, you've got to learn how to have your own back and you've got to get SUPER EXCITED about YOU ...About your life and all of the possibilities that await you. You've got to get SUPER EXCITED about your plans and dreams and give your life everything you've got. You've got to get SUPER EXCITED about the woman who you are becoming and evolving into. YOU haven't even scratched the surface of all of your *Magnificence* yet. This is why you must date you.

Grab A Girlfriend and Go Live Your Dreams by Cassandra Mack

Today, think about a date that you would like to take yourself on. Plan it and do it. And don't forget to wear something spectacular.

☑ **Your Reminder** – Love yourself! Embrace your magnificence and take yourself on a date this week.

⮑ **Repeat This Aloud** – *Today I am going to plan a great date for myself. I will dress up, get excited and do something I've always wanted to do. I am learning to not only enjoy my own company but I am also getting acquainted with my deepest desires and secret longings in a way that feels wonderful.*

🖋 **Journaling** - Reflect on the lessons learned from day 28 of the *Grab A Girlfriend and Go Live Your Dreams* 30-day challenge. Pick up a notepad or journal to be used exclusively for this 30-day program and write down at least one thing that you can do today to put the lessons learned from today's reading into practice. Use your journal to make any notes-to-self, journal your thoughts and feelings about today's task or jot down anything else that you feel prompted to write concerning your *Grab A Girlfriend and Go Live Your Dreams* journey.

Day 29.
Don't Be Afraid To Make
A FOOL of Yourself
Forget. Other. Opinions. & Leap.

You are never going to unleash your greatness and achieve your biggest, boldest dreams if you don't put yourself out there. STRETCH YOURSELF like you've never stretched before and do something that makes you feel a little foolish. If you're afraid to make a fool of yourself, then you will hold yourself back because you won't take the necessary BIG, BOLD risks to make your dreams come true. Being afraid to look foolish has held more people back from achieving their biggest, boldest dreams than lack of talent, lack of discipline and virtually any other thing you could possibly think of. Are you willing to play the fool for your dreams?

Many singers were discovered because they risked looking foolish by singing in subway stations. Many comedians were discovered because they risked looking foolish by performing on street corners and rinky, dinky dumps in order to perfect their craft and gain exposure. Many authors sold lots of books because they rejected conventional wisdom and did something so out of the box that they risked looking foolish. Many people who are living their dreams now are only successful because they were willing to do something that others might consider unabashed, or foolish. So what am I saying? Simply this: *Are you willing to make a fool of yourself in order to achieve your dreams?*

Billionaire Richard Branson, who is the founder of Virgin Atlantic Airways, referenced his mentor when he said these words: "*At the time, I was running a little record company; I was about 17 years old. The first time I met one of my greatest mentors was some years later. I was thinking about setting up my own airline*, when my mentor gave me this advice: "*You'll never have the advertising power to outsell British Airways. You are going to have to get out there and use yourself. Make a fool of yourself. Otherwise you won't survive.*" In essence what his mentor was saying was this: In order to do something great you must be willing to do something that not only takes you out of your comfort zone but that scares the hell out of you.

Walt Disney, Oprah, Madonna, Lady Ga Ga, Tyler Perry, Serena Williams, Sean Puffy Combs all stretched themselves to the point of looking foolish. They took a chance on themselves and they won. They risked looking crazy, foolish and stupid. They risked being talked about, laughed at and rejected. And then they shook it off, took a deep breath...and then a leap of FAITH. And in the end, they all had the last laugh.

With this in mind: Where can it be said that you are going to have to **F**orget **O**ther **O**pinions and **L**eap?

☑ **Your Reminder** – Give yourself the gift of looking foolish. Don't be afraid to put yourself

135

out there and risk looking foolish for your dreams.

◔ **Repeat This Aloud** – *I am willing to risk looking stupid, crazy and foolish in order to achieve my biggest, boldest dreams.*

✎   **Journaling** - Reflect on the lessons learned from day 29 of the *Grab A Girlfriend and Go Live Your Dreams* 30-day challenge. Pick up a notepad or journal to be used exclusively for this 30-day program and write down at least one thing that you can do today to put the lessons learned from today's reading into practice. Use your journal to make any notes-to-self, journal your thoughts and feelings about today's task or jot down anything else that you feel prompted to write concerning your *Grab A Girlfriend and Go Live Your Dreams* journey.

Day 30.
Make A Video of Yourself Taking A Leap of Faith

Guess what? You made it all the way to the end. You are on day 30 of the *Grab A Girlfriend and Go Live Your Dreams* challenge. I am super, duper proud of you. I am beaming with pride, giving you a big high-five.

Today we are putting it all together ...all of the hard work you've done, all of the self-doubt and fear that you've pushed through, all of the passion and purpose that you have released in your life, all of the great ideas that you've got percolating in your head and are about to manifest in a monumental way.

Now it's time for you to take a leap of faith towards your dreams. In my previous book, *Grab A Girlfriend and Go Take Your Life Back,* I talked about a concept known as *going public,* where you put yourself out there by sharing one of your goals on social media so that everyone who knows you knows what you are trying to accomplish and can hold you accountable as well as encourage you to go for it.

Just like companies go public, people can go public too. The beauty about going public is that once you put it out there, there is no turning back. For example: If you tell everyone you know that you're running a marathon, and if you post it on a popular social networking site you can rest assured that people are going to ask you how it's going, perhaps every time they see you. As a

Grab A Girlfriend and Go Live Your Dreams by Cassandra Mack

result you'll be more inclined to stick with it, even if you feel like quitting.

Here's what you gain by going public: You gain support from others. More importantly, you gain the expectation from those that know about your big goal that you are going to see it through. You'll be held accountable. You'll have people encouraging you and cheering you on. You'll also motivate other people who never thought they could live their dreams until they see someone just like you living yours.

When you pursue your dreams as a lone wolf, you often lose sight of the fact that you are doing the most important thing in your life: becoming the best version of yourself. But with the support of others people, you'll be more inclined to keep on keeping on even when life gets hectic and crazy.

Here's the other piece: If you don't go public with your big ideas and dreams, then you are not giving your life the fair chance that it deserves. Although going public puts you in the hot seat it also puts you in the driver's seat of your life.

So here's your assignment for today: Today you are going to make a short video of yourself taking a leap of faith towards your dreams. You are going to post this video on Facebook and Youtube with the hash tag **#GrabAGirlfriendandGoLiveYourDreams** make sure to tag me in it.

There is no right or wrong way to make your video, as long as it represents you taking a leap of faith towards your dreams. It can be a video of you singing or dancing or writing or going to an office supply store to purchase supplies for

138

that business that you want to start. It can be a video of you researching the licenses and permits you'll need for a particular business. It can be a video of you standing in front of the college that you want to attend or of you driving through a neighborhood that you want to purchase a home in or a video of you at a home buying seminar. It can be a video of you calling a hotel to inquire about the cost to host your special event there, or a video of you cooking, baking, painting, gardening or showing off your handmade jewelry or styling someone's hair and nails or applying make-up. It can be a video of you at a conference for authors if you're an aspiring author or of you giving a tutorial about a subject you want to teach in your business. It can be a video of you reading a page from your forthcoming book or stage play. Your video can be anything you want it to be as long as it shows you taking a leap of faith towards your dreams. Have fun with it.

Let's do a quick 4-step review of what you're going to do
.

1. Make a short video of yourself taking a leap of faith towards your dreams using the hash tag **#GrabAGirlfriendandGoLiveYouDreams**

2. At the start of your video, state your name, city and state. Reference the book, *Grab A Girlfriend & Go Live Your Dreams* by Cassandra Mack. Also tell us what your dream is.

3. Explain how, what you're doing in your video is a leap of faith towards your dreams.

For example: Hi my name is... I'm from (blank) city and state. I just took Cassandra Mack's Grab A Girlfriend & Go Live Your Dreams 30-Day Challenge....
And I am taking a leap of faith towards my dreams. My dream is to start my own catering business. In this video I am making five German Chocolate Cakes for my child's school. This is a leap of faith for me because I have never publicly shared this dream of mine or baked for a group this size before....

4. Upload your video to YouTube and your Facebook page. Don't forget to tag me on it and use the hash tag **#GrabAGirlfriendandGoLiveYourDreams**

☑ **Your Reminder** – Take a leap of faith towards your dreams and make your video.

➲ **Repeat This Aloud** – *I am excited about creating my leap of faith video. I will have fun with this.*

🖉 **Journaling** - Reflect on the lessons learned from day 30 of the *Grab A Girlfriend and Go Live Your Dreams* 30-day challenge. Pick up a notepad or journal to be used exclusively for this 30-day program and write down at least one thing that you can do today to put the lessons learned from today's reading into practice. Use your journal to make any notes-to-self, journal your thoughts and feelings about today's task or jot down anything else that you feel prompted to write concerning your *Grab A Girlfriend and Go Live Your Dreams* journey.

Self Check-In

✓ What have you accomplished thus far, since doing the *Grab A Girlfriend and Go Live Your Dreams* 30 day challenge? *(either big or small)*

✓ How do you feel right now about the progress you've made thus far?

✓ Was there any part of the program that you were struggling to follow-thru on? If yes, why were you struggling with that particular part of the challenge?

✓ Write down one thing that you can do this week to move your life one step closer to living your dreams.

Girlfriend Check-In

We've come to the last girlfriend check-in. Even though this is the last check-in in this book, you can continue checking in with your girlfriend on your own as you carry on with your dream. Don't forget to have a pen and notebook readily available so that you can jot down any helpful ideas or suggestions that come out of your girlfriend check-in.

Summarize 3 things that you did this week to move your life in the direction that you want it to go in. Talk about any challenges you faced. Ask for feedback. Now that you've come to the end of the book, what are your next steps moving forward?

_____

_____

_____

_____

_____

_____

_____

_____

_____

_____

_____

_____

Grab A Girlfriend and Go Live Your Dreams by Cassandra Mack

Dream Work Check List

1. Create Daily Success Routines

2. Think On Paper

3. Let Your Highest Values Serve As Your Guideposts

4. Remember That Every Step Counts

5. Let Go of Habits That Do Not Serve You Well

6. Be Willing To Wash A Few Backs

7. Get The Inside Scoop On Your Dreams

8. Date Yourself Like You Would Date An Individual Who You Were Super Excited About

9. Don't Be Afraid To Make A F.O.O.L. of Yourself

10.   Make A Video of Yourself Taking A Leap Of Faith

Grab A Girlfriend and Go Live Your Dreams by Cassandra Mack

My Closing Words To You

Living your dreams is all about building a life around your deepest desires and heartfelt longings. Living your dreams is about building a life that is reflective of your true *Magnificence, Brilliance* and *Authenticity*. Living your dreams is about never saying *NEVER* and never saying that it's too late. Living your dreams is about recognizing and realizing that your VOICE is worth being heard and your PASSIONS are worth pursuing. Living your dreams is about purpose, personal power and possibility.

And when we push fear out of the way and live and breathe our dreams; the possibilities for our lives are endless. You are a leader, a creator and a beautiful dreamer. Never forget how powerful you are. Thank you for allowing me to serve as your personal coach for the *Grab A Girlfriend & Go Live Your Dreams* 30-Day challenge.

You took the first step by completing the *Grab A Girlfriend and Go Live Your Dreams* 30 day challenge, with me as your personal coach ....guiding you, prompting you and pushing you to grow forward. Now the rest is up to you. You have what it takes to not only make it but to manifest your dreams in a way that feels right for your life. I'll be rooting for you.

Always Remember – *You hold the pen that writes the chapters of your life. And when you grab a girlfriend and go...YOU don't have to go it alone.*

See you at the top!

Grab A Girlfriend and Go Live Your Dreams by Cassandra Mack

Want to stay in touch with me?

Website:
www.strategiesforempoweredliving.com

Twitter:
Twitter.com/theCassandraMac

Facebook:
Facebook.com/StrategiesforEmpoweredLivingWithCassandraMack

Youtube:
Youtube.com/user/CassandraMackchannel.

Bring A Cassandra Mack Keynote or Workshop To Your Event or Organization

Are you an HR Director or executive facing an organizational or employee challenge within your company that needs to be addressed and explored? Cassandra Mack has helped hundreds of individuals, nonprofit organizations and government agencies develop effective ways to deal with workplace issues that impact performance and productivity. Executives, HR and Organizational Development directors have used Cassandra Mack to tackle some of the most common challenges that plague work environments, such as: ineffective or toxic communication, low team morale, workplace conflict, lack of productivity, misalignment about roles on a team, leading others towards their best success and how to coach, counsel and mentor employees for maximum productivity.

From leadership development for your executive level managers and supervisory skills for new supervisors to professionalism and personal effectiveness for your entire team; Cassandra Mack can work with your organization to help you achieve your desired results. Whether you want to maximize the diverse gifts and talents of your leaders; equip your front-line staff with the essential skills to align with vision, build team cohesion, communicate better, boost morale or adapt well to new changes, Cassandra Mack can assist you. Cassandra Mack's educational courses and professional development learning programs will help you reach your goals faster and empower your staff to do their jobs with greater skill, ease and effectiveness.

Grab A Girlfriend and Go Live Your Dreams by Cassandra Mack

Following are 7 Benefits to bringing a Cassandra Mack Training Program to your organization:

1. Increase the collective knowledge of your entire team when they have vastly different viewpoints and work styles that hinder staff alignment and team cohesion.
2. Help your employees function better interpersonally so that managers spend less time refereeing conflicts and miscommunication and more time maximizing their team members and resources.
3. Groom future leaders for your organization. When a manager leaves the company, there is often a decline in productivity due to the company not being able to fill the position with a qualified candidate. But with targeted training now, you can help ensure your current workforce is prepared to seamlessly move up the ladder as needed.
4. Enable managers/supervisors to develop a better assessment of their employees' strengths, professional goals and developmental needs consequently maximizing employee retention and growth.
5. Better prepare your employees to develop interpersonal agility skills in order to deal with the changing demands of the workplace and business environment.
6. Align employees conduct, work habits and professional practices with the culture, mission and vision of your organization as well as the goals of each department within your company.
7. Make it easier for your organization to know where to plan, budget and allocate resources by evaluating the outcome of the training.

   ➢ For more information about Cassandra Mack's training courses go to:
   StrategiesForEmpoweredLiving.com

Grab A Girlfriend and Go Live Your Dreams by Cassandra Mack

Private Coaching With Cassandra Mack

Whenever we step into a new season of life, or move into higher realms of responsibility or we want to experience greater success and effectiveness in a particular area of our lives; we must develop new tools, skills and strategies to take us where we want to go. When we have the right knowledge, the right framework, the right strategies and the right tools we become empowered to achieve our goals with greater ease and we are better prepared to step into the task that we are about to embark on with clarity confidence and competence.

The real value of being in a coaching relationship with a life coach who is bible-based is twofold: First, the Bible is the primary framework that undergirds the coaching sessions. Second the tips, tools and tactics that we will utilize together will be in alignment with your foundational beliefs and faith.

Whether you want to focus on leadership development, your relationships or your emotional well-being, coaching with Cassandra Mack will help you get unstuck, create a sustainable plan to help you achieve your desired results and provide you with strategies to move your life in the direction that you want to go in with greater clarity, confidence, and effectiveness.

What makes coaching with Cassandra Mack, exceptionally beneficial is, Cassandra bridges the psychology of success, the dynamics of human behavior, and timeless Biblical principles with her innovative empowerment strategies and 17 plus years of successful experience as an executive coach, master facilitator, social worker and thought leader to help individuals and organization build capacity and enhance wellbeing. As a result, Cassandra Mack offers her clients a deeper understanding of what's driving their behavior, what's hindering their success and how to tap their inner strengths and unrealized potential which in turn enables them to achieve their goals faster and utilize her unique techniques to make their lives better.

Grab A Girlfriend and Go Live Your Dreams by Cassandra Mack

➤ Are you ready to live a more inspired, and intentional life? Try a coaching session with Cassandra Mack and start seizing your success and repositioning yourself for victorious living. For more information go to: **StrategiesForEmpoweredLiving.com**

If You Enjoyed This Book
Leave A Review On Amazon

If you enjoyed this book or received value from it in any way, then I'd like to ask you for a favor: would you be kind enough to leave a review for this book on Amazon? It'd be greatly appreciated! Your Amazon reviews help to get this book into more hands that need to hear this message. Thank you.

Grab A Girlfriend and Go Live Your Dreams by Cassandra Mack

Other Books By Cassandra Mack

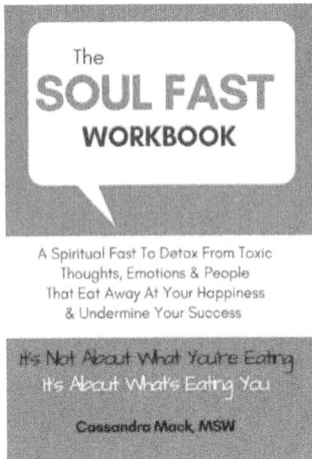

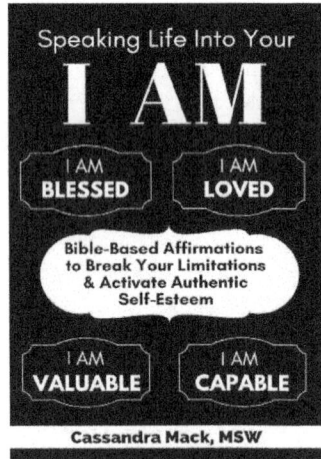

Grab A Girlfriend and Go Live Your Dreams by Cassandra Mack

Made in the USA
Monee, IL
28 January 2021